Love,
PAPÁ

A Book to My Children

JESÚS ZUBIATE

Cover Photograph by: João Machado

PAGE PUBLISHING, INC.
Conneaut Lake, PA

First originally published by Page Publishing 2020

ISBN 978-1-6624-3103-6 (pbk)
ISBN 978-1-6624-3104-3 (digital)

Printed in the United States of America

To my children, who with their smiles, love, and temper tantrums
have inspired me to write in faith and with a joyful heart.

No discipline seems pleasant at the time, but painful.
Later on, however, it produces a harvest of righteousness
and pace for those who have been trained by it.

—Hebrews 12:11

CONTENTS

PREFACE

WHEN THE BLESSING of having children came into our lives, I found myself looking for ways to accompany them throughout their journey even after God marks the end of my days on this earth. Full of wisdom, my mother would say, "Ink has a more powerful memory than our mind." I leave my heart and soul on these pages with the hope that it instills in my children and readers the love of God.

In the years I spent writing this book, I searched deeply within the labyrinths of my mind, looking for coherent ways to articulate my memories on paper. I wrote this novel for my children based on my personal journey to seek a fulfilled life in the midst of challenging seasons. From my childhood in Mexico to my years in the United States, I was inspired by the grace of God and His unrelenting patience and love. I found the courage to translate my thoughts into words by the support of my graceful and tenacious wife, who stood by my side through every word that was written in this book.

This book is a celebration of the many hardships and life circumstances that we each face in our own journey to whichever goal our hearts desire. It is a reminder that no matter the struggle, God is in control.

PART 1

CHAPTER 1

The Miracle of *Futbol*

IT WAS THE middle of summer in the late eighties, or it could have been any day of any season in my childhood life. I remember the drilling Mexican sun eating away at my cracked, dry cheeks. My cheeks would dry out with the never-ending bright sun and dust that swirled through the hot desert city. I remember my mother always chasing me around with that greasy petroleum product to rub on my face. My mother's daily goal was to have children with soft and hydrated cheeks. "What will people say about the parents of a kid with dry cheeks? They are going to say that their mother does not take care of her children! No! Not in my house, not about my children," my mother would say.

As a kid, I never understood the logic behind it, but it certainly made me pay attention to other kids' cheeks. I always noticed that many kids had white spots on their cheeks. My mother always said that it was because of "all that bad candy they would eat" and that candy was not nutritious for the body and even less for the skin. Frankly, I do not remember a lot of kids eating candy. Actually, most of them barely had any meals throughout the day, and I distinctly remember the odor of old dry beans in their mouths. Now I know my mother was somehow right about her comments. The white spots in part were a sign of malnutrition, but not because of excessive candy but instead because of continuous hunger as a result of our impoverished state of living.

But on this particular day, the dry cheeks and white spots or the bad breath of children around me was not one of my worries. That day we had the last game out of a series of games that were played for ten consecutive days. While street soccer was a year-round sport, this day was different. The only obstacle between the championship and me was a shoeless beehive of kids and a couple of old junk cars. The glory of triumph could be reached between a couple of rocks marking the goal. In previous times, we would use metal trash cans as goal posts, but moving them every time a car would pass was extremely annoying and laborious, especially if the trash cans were full and under extreme street-dog supervision. The great majority of dogs on the dirty, semipaved, bumpy, and dusty street where I grew up were the furthest away from pets. They were scruffy territorial animals shaped by scarcity, neglect, and abuse.

They were free, yet slaves to their street for their own safety. They worked in packs, reverting to their wolf ancestry and assumed a vigilante role in each and every street throughout the city. They were not owned; they were not pampered or loved or wanted. Dogs in my street were multiplying wild animals surviving on scraps from the trash and seldom by the kindness of a Good Samaritan.

Consequently, any of the few available rusty, dented trash cans were always property of the street pack. Especially those cans that provided the most desired food on the street menu, baby diapers.

On that day, we kept it simple: two rocks as the goal, whoever gets to ten goals is the winner, and no dogs were allowed as team members. In full disagreement, my dog Lobo, who was one of the only dog pets on the street living outside in our patio, sat tied to a crooked old post light. Several barks throughout the game and his whimpering served only to inspire and cheer on the team. Even the best players get benched in special circumstances. It was Lobo's destiny to watch the game from the post this time because of past mistakes or well-known dog faults. If only he did not try to bite Jose after he took the ball from him during the last game, then Lobo would not have missed the championship game for improper, aggressive player behavior and a well-deserved imaginary red card.

Our street had been paved when we moved in, but the engineers did not install a proper sewer system, so the tar had to be demolished and semirepaired. The good news was that there was less dust in the house and our cheeks were healthier. Not to mention the house was cleaner. Less dust meant less hours for my mom cleaning every single corner of the house. "What will people think if they walk into a dusty house? They will think we are a dirty family with an irresponsible mother. No, not in my house." My mom and the neighbors were mad at the shoddy job, but thankful that we were lucky enough to have some type of sewer and paving. Most of them grew up without either. Everyone knew the money to fix the street was kept by the politicians, and once the rich people got involved, we could not do much about it. Silence would not fix the injustices but at least would keep you out of trouble. So we all turned around and kept on living our lives like nothing ever happened.

On that day, even with the imposed soccer rules of the day, several rules did not change. We also had the same old patched, deflated, and dirty plastic ball. It was hard to keep a ball inflated and in pristine shape given the exposure to the half-paved roads and passing cars always running them over. There was no hope for a good ball. We tried basketballs, which were extremely hard to kick, volleyballs, and even a baseball, which was very small and would hurt our toes. To maintain a ball in good shape, we went to the extremes. We knew that getting a new one was close to impossible, so we cleaned it and even slept right next to it to ensure its security. Once the ball went bad and deflated, we even touched on the basics of chemistry. We exposed it to the sun for dense air that could reinflate it and even experimented with liquids. Soda, for instance, was responsible for successful patches. All we needed to do was somehow put some Coke inside the ball and let it dry. But even without a ball, the game never stopped. We were the MacGyvers of soccer. Our lifestyles forced us to be creative and clever. A couple of days' worth of the neighbor's newspapers and some stolen tape from my mom's teaching drawer were the perfect materials to make a ball, and the game continued. There was nothing in the world like the game of soccer. Our feet were hard and thick, our skills always improving, and life hid behind the screams of goal after goal.

The street was not any different on that day. There was the same old car from the grumpy neighbor, always parked in the same place, making our field smaller. This one car bothered us greatly because we knew it could be moved for the sake of a proper soccer field. It almost felt like our grumpy neighbor wanted to intentionally shrink our playing space. However, there were other cars without tires and laying on bricks that had been parked there for years. There was no hope to move those anywhere, so we worked our way around them and even used them as bouncing walls to strike dream passes.

The team was the same again. With so many kids on the street, we kept it simple: we divided the north side from the south side. Sometimes, however, strange alliances would form, and a couple of kids would join the rival team. No hard feelings as long as we had the same number of kids on each team. There were days when the numbers were uneven, but I was always willing to play for the team with fewer players. To me, it was a challenge and would only help my soccer skills.

On this day, we were even. Same team for a few days now, and I had played every single game of the week. Usually, I would miss a day here and there. My mom would never let me play before finishing my homework and would not let me go out if it was too late, so priorities after school were very clear: clean your dusty shoes, hang and fold your uniform, help with the chores, eat, and get to your homework. My mom would complain that she would never get any help and that all I wanted to do was play on the street. Guilty I was—I would finish things as soon as possible and round the kids out to the street.

Somehow, I was the only kid with responsibilities. Everyone else would come out and play anytime. I used to think my mother was very mean with me. How dare she not let me play like the other kids! "Why, Mom? Why can everyone else go out and you never let me?" I screamed. My mom replied by saying, "One day you will understand, son." It was even harder for me because most kids would also play at school. I tried it once and got spanked so hard that I did not do it again. The problem was not the game but the shoes and the uniform. My mom struggled to afford one pair of shoes for me to go to school with, and these shoes were not to be wrecked "for a few kicks." I was not allowed to play in the one pair I had, so barefoot I went, but never at school. Being the son of a teacher, I was always to look clean and well put together. Taking my shoes off to play at school was unacceptable. Not to mention that washing my uniform every day by hand was a lot of work for my mom. I remember my mom scrubbing our clothes on the washing board every afternoon and dreaming of the day that she could afford a washer—almost an impossible dream. I can close my eyes and see my mother's wrinkly hands, with her fingers so pruned that they were nearly split open.

Neither the lack of shoes nor the lack of a place to play nor having a ball were reasons to give up on the game. We were fulfilled kids chasing taped newspaper around barefoot on a crooked road, dodging cars, dodging life, watching out for dog bites, and it all seemed normal.

As my dog barked, almost pushing me to do my best in the game, I took that old ball and drilled down a few kids before facing the last standing player. As if it was destiny for the neighbor to park his car in that place on that day, I bounced the ball off the door as a pass to myself and scored the final goal.

Professional athletes raise their gold medals and trophies, make fortunes, and make the news all over the world. They even come out in commercials as part of history. On this day, I did not win a trophy, any money, nor a gold medal. I'm pretty sure I did not even gain the neighbor's approval as I bounced the old ball off his car, but I found utopia as a cracked, deflated old ball crossed the chosen rocks. My goal did not make the news, and unfortunately, I cannot show you a replay; but in the labyrinth of my memory, street soccer wins and goals remind me of the feeling of joy and happiness. These moments marked my childhood and allowed me to begin to understand and differentiate the feeling of joy from the feeling of the painful, traumatic life my family and I were living. Our life was not normal.

CHAPTER 2

A Laborious Childhood

IT WAS THE winter of the early nineties. I was an eight-year-old already thinking as a young adult. The struggles at home and our lifestyle had built a unique type of wisdom that eight-year-olds do not have, should not have. It was a wisdom that vanished my innocent childhood thoughts and removed much needed filters that take away worries from a child. This is the filter that I see on you, my children, when you smile at the simple sound of my clapping and silly faces. The beautiful lenses through which you view Christmas as a magical time and do not require a scientific explanation about Santa Claus's ability to fly his sled.

At age eight, while other kids played and dreamed of Santa going down the chimney at night, I stressed about the source of food and the ability of my mother to make Christmas magical for my siblings and being able to afford presents. The worst part was worrying about my father's behavior. Christmas nights, like many other nights, were stained by his drunkenness and aggressive behavior. Instead of enjoying Christmas, I would pray for my father to not drink on that night, and I prayed even harder that he would not show up at all. I clearly remember praying for angels to set camp around our house. With an accelerated heartbeat pounding in my chest and uncontainable anxiety weakening my legs, knowing that my father would show up anytime, I prayed that he would not hurt us. I prayed that angels would guard our door and that somehow my father's threats that would keep playing in my head would not become a reality. "You keep siding with your mother, and one day I will burn you and everyone in this house while you are asleep," he would say to me. What kind of monster threatens his young boy with death and pain for innocently trying to defend his mother? I was a boy with insignificant physical strength against the rage of a drunken man. My father's actions are incomprehensible and inexcusable.

* * *

My children, I often dwell on such hurtful memories as I look and feel your beautiful, tiny, and squishy hands. My heart, yet again, beats fast and pounds in my chest, but this time it is out of love and joy to have you as my children. Your smiles, your signature movements and milestones, and the implausible miracle of having you in my life and being able to enjoy the gift of fatherhood are a true blessing.

* * *

At age eight, I learned that our local market store was hiring bagging boys. Against my mother's will and fully coherent about the purpose of my actions, which was to be able to help her with an income, I applied and was hired. It was not hard to make a good impression on people at that age. My mother worked hard at instilling good manners in us. She also worked hard at helping keep a clean presentation. "Being poor is not an excuse for being dirty. Poor and dirty are not the same thing," my mother would say all the time. Even at eight years old, a pair of old but polished shoes, a firm handshake, and direct eye contact was able to get me a job. But as young as one may think the age of eight may be to have a job, bagging groceries was not the first job I ever had, nor had it been the youngest that I had a job. I must have been three or four years old when my great-grandfather would take me out to help him execute the last job he ever had in his last years of life. Certainly an ironic situation: it was my great-grandfather who gave me my very first job helping him with his last one. This was a job that required nothing more than a strong, loud, and compelling voice. I was the yelling voice, the human speaker of his street orange sales business. My great-grandfather had raised sixteen children working the land under all-weather conditions his entire life. But in the last years of his life, unable to work as hard, he unleashed his entrepreneurial spirit. He bought an old cargo tricycle with a metal platform big enough to carry oranges and slowly pedaled through the streets selling them. My great-grandfather was a tall strong man. His skin had been broken by the sun and wrinkled in untraceable patterns. Nevertheless, there was not a single wrinkle traced incorrectly or without a meaning. It was like his face could tell you many stories without speaking a single word or showing any expression. His eyes were like the color of a foggy morning. In fact, there was no color in them, only a strange but kind emptiness. The incongruent shades of his dark bronzed skin were like the work of a bad artist who never took the time to blend his colors.

As a young boy he outlived the Mexican Revolution and never knew anything else but hard work. I can still close my eyes and see his shaky, wrinkled, aged fingers holding to the handles of the old tricycle with his hazy and tired eyes. Aside from the oranges, we would carry a cutting board with a sharp sticky knife, chili powder, and salt. We sold juicy oranges with enough chili powder to spice up the flavor of those hot afternoons. Our marketing approach was very simple but extremely laborious for my young vocal cords. "ORANGES, ORANGES! COME OUT, COME OUT! HERE COME THE FRESH ORANGES!" I yelled as my great-grandfather slowly pedaled the tricycle with his tired legs. However, oftentimes my voice was not loud enough to attract customers, so I deployed my second marketing technique: I knocked on every single door one at a time, offering juicy, spicy oranges until our sales goals were reached. With another day behind us, a monetary payment was not the manner of compensation. Instead, my great-grandfather paid me well with unlimited oranges. Many were the afternoons when I sat on that pile of oranges and licked my sticky, dirty fingers with a full belly after a hard afternoon of work. The few but very clear memories that I have of these beautiful days bring me happiness. It was at a very young age that my great-grandfather, perhaps unintentionally, planted the very first seed of work ethic and perseverance.

My eighth winter as a young boy was very prosperous. School was out for vacation, and I was bagging groceries three to four hours per day. The money was good. Fanny packs were a great resource for the job. The bigger the fanny pack, the more coins it could fit. Each client would tip me a few coins for bagging their groceries, and the faster I was, the more money I would make. Picking a fast cashier was a fundamental move, so I, intelligently, showed up early every day to pick the best person to team up with. With Christmas around the corner, the lines were long and my fanny pack heavier. It was like a pirate coin treasure, with coins of all sizes and colors and even a few bills from touched clients who were generous as a result of the season. There were probably fifteen kids per shift, and I am certain that I was not the youngest. But age did not matter, we were all a cocktail of broken homes and tough backgrounds. Not all of us had good hearts either. We all knew about the many knife assaults when kids would steal money from each other. We also had the typical bully kid who would take money from other kids by sheer intimidation. We even had to be careful of adult thieves who would patiently wait for our shift to be over and assault us on our way home. But we all had the common goal of helping our households, and while for many it was not a matter of choice to work, we all did our best to fill our fanny packs and pockets with money—fifteen kids in an improvised uniform that consisted of a white collared shirt and black pants. I remember the old translucent shirts that most kids would wear, so translucent that one could see their skin and so far from white that one could swear they were yellow. Most kids had discolored spots on their faces and stained teeth. One could see the hunger and struggle in their eyes and in their dry, cracked skin. We were fighters, survivors graduated from the school of life with honors at a very young age. We were young and relentless. We had a job instead of toys; we were on a mission and not on a dream.

At the end of each shift, I would go home in joy. Some days I walked, which would take me about thirty minutes; and some other days, I would take the local bus, which would only charge a few coins. I would get home and give my earnings to my mother, who would use part of it and save the rest. The small savings were helpful for school supplies and uniforms. The rest was a blessing for food or anything needed at the house. One great memory of those days is when I decided to buy groceries right after my shift. I remember navigating the aisles of the store, buying groceries and a gift for each of my siblings and my mother. It had been a great day of earnings. I remember the grocery bags were so heavy for my small body after I went through the register that I candidly decided to take a taxi home. I laugh as tears fill my eyes when I think of that day. I was an eight-year-old walking through each store aisle in search of goods, toys, and for my mother, a beautiful coffee mug. I learned at a very young age that receiving will never compare with giving. This basic concept was no different than our Christmas mornings, when my siblings would wake up to the humble presents that my mother and I had placed under the Christmas tree in the name of Santa. As happy as my siblings' eyes were, they could not compare to my mother's quiet, hidden tears of joy. Another year had gone by, and God had never abandoned us. My siblings and I kept growing, and life had much more ahead of us.

Not all memories of my childhood are charitable like my shopping spree after a long day of work. In my childhood, meat was not part of our daily diets. I still remember sneaking in the kitchen quietly when the day would come and secretly steal pieces of meat from the delicious soups my mom would cook. I knew the serving would only have a few pieces, so my selfish instinct would make me engage in premeal sampling behaviors. I feel guilty now, as I write about it, but my heart shatters in pieces as the memories of my mom serving our food comes to mind. "Why aren't you eating, Mom?" I used to ask. "I am not hungry right now, son," she would say. Yet the pan was empty already after serving our rations. What a fool I was, chewing and savoring that tasty meal in front of my mother, who with tired and joyful eyes, filled her hunger with our smiles in approval of a tasty meal. I want to scream to that selfish boy; I want to slap him and shake him and help him read what is taking place and split my plate and give half to my mother. I want to place wisdom in his mind and help him mature quickly enough to the point where his mother cannot lie to him and pretend she is not hungry. I want to stop feeling this painful regret for not reading each moment correctly and taking action. But that is the love of a mother: unconditional, endless, pure, the closest to God Himself and the furthest from selfish.

At eight years old, bagging groceries was not my only source of income. I remember always thinking about different ways to make money for the house and oftentimes coming up with ingenious ideas. One recurring technique that did not need much planning or strategizing was taking advantage of my father's drunkenness. His behavior was very volatile while drunk. However, when he had exhausted his rage and outpaced his drinking endurance, he would fall asleep deeply. It was during this time that I would slowly search his pockets looking for leftover coins or bills. I knew his drunkenness would never allow him to remember how much money he went to sleep with, so I took advantage of it. Of course, I am not proud of such actions, but in our position, such a petty crime would be justified by the needs. A gallon of milk, eggs, tortillas, or any food to put on the table was worth the risk.

But not all my ideas required an illegal act like pocket theft. The raffle strategy was one of my most successful business strategies and worth writing about. This strategy could only be executed with relentless determination, hard work and a targeted marketing strategy. Living in a teachers' house always gave me access to some type of school supplies. My mother always kept additional pens or notepads that she would use for her class planning and sometimes to give away to kids who could not afford it. With such access to these types of resources, I had a very simple idea. I built a raffle system where I could give away notepads and pens and other miscellaneous items like erasers and more. My raffle program was very appealing as only a few cents could get a kid multiple materials for school. I even came up with a slogan: "Back-to-school package." But to create a raffle one needs tickets to sell. To accomplish this easy task, I would cut small paper squares of about two by two inches, each with a handwritten number on it, usually as high as 300. My goal was to sell as many numbers as possible for a good return on investment. The most challenging part of my plan was acquiring clients. Therefore, I walked many miles during multiple days, knocking on many doors and avoiding many heartless dogs who thought of me as an intruder and not a business boy. Of the hundreds of doors I knocked on, some of them opened up, allowing for my pragmatic pitch: "Hi, ma'am. I am selling tickets for an amazing raffle that could get one of your kids most of the materials that he or she needs for going back to school! The best part is that it will only cost you a fraction of the price that you would pay if you buy this whole package." I would then show them the prize, which was really a bag with a few notepads and pens. The days were long as I walked the many dusty streets. The sun felt like sandpaper, rubbing my body and darkening anything on me that was exposed. The heat would draw all the sweat out of my pores during those long walks, but never my determination. My fears and emotions walked those streets with me as I was constantly chased by dogs and most doors were shut closed. I remember pausing my walks behind the skinny shade of lamp poles to give my body a break. One pole after the other fed my hope to rest with the well-measured distance between them.

* * *

Children, it is not until one faces the deepest struggle that we humbly and thankfully learn to appreciate the most insignificant things in life, like the ignored shade of a streetlight pole—the same shade that patiently waited for me on each street to give aid to my dehydrated body. Whether you find yourself in the middle of scarcity or abundance, never stop thanking the Lord, never stop paying attention to the most insignificant things in life, big or small; they all come from God. Do not long for what you cannot have just yet or will never have. Instead, be thankful, enjoy, and get the most of what has been given to you already. Look at the birds, at how cheerfully, relentlessly, and gratefully they build their nests one pine needle at a time. With vision and determination, one can build castles out of mud and find joy and gratefulness in the forgotten treasures that God has given us.

* * *

With the earnings of the raffle, I would replace the materials and the money for house needs. But raffles, bagging groceries, and searching in my drunken father's pockets was not all I ever did. I collected cardboard, cans, and anything of value that I could resell. I kept an eye on opportunities, and above all, I impatiently waited for the time when I could have an adult job. I spent my childhood worrying about basic needs, dreaming about the future but boldly aware of the present. I don't know that I clearly understood that there were other lifestyles. I might have caught a glimpse of it in observing other people's lives, but preoccupied with my own, I seldom had the time to stop and meditate about it. Every day was a repetition of the last one with a light variation. Yes, I played. Yes, I laughed and ran and kicked a ball like a kid, but the outcome would always be the same. We lived a fearful life, a limited life—a life full of disappointments, tragedy, abuse. And somehow in the middle of such a chronic storm stood a loving mother who did not relent—a mother who taught us respect, values and morals, and most importantly, the word of God. Cold or hot, rain or shine, we were in church every Sunday. We walked, we rushed, we ran, we went in the bus or in a car when we had one, four clean and fed children raised by this unbreakable faith. She was a love machine, a farmer who diligently planted and watered the seed of God, the seed of hope, perseverance, and resilience. God never abandoned us, and even in the middle of the chaos, His plan was in effect; He was always in control.

CHAPTER 3

Rage

IT WAS NOT long before time, and its waiting tricks could no longer stop me from becoming a young adult. My childhood had passed, and I found myself getting older or at least perceiving myself to be older. The many struggles and storms had already scarred me, but at the time, I felt mentally healthy. Education where I grew up, while it is a right during the first six years, is not free or available like the laws proudly state it is. Laws vaguely support a model where children receive a so-called free education until sixth grade, which is the end of primary or elementary school. Everyone knows that on paper and for purposes of appearances and deceitful reporting, children go to primary school without the need to pay a penny out of pocket. But in reality, many children go through life without learning how to read and write as a result of their family's economic status. I could have been part of this statistic as well if my life would have been in my father's hands only. I would have never attended even primary school and would have been deprived of basic needs like shelter and food. But my mother made sure that her four children built a life foundation upheld by education.

In Mexico, after sixth grade, to pursue the next level of education, children must earn their spot in the few available schools. After sixth grade, because of the overwhelming number of students and the limited number of secondary schools, all students must earn their way in through an academic exam.

This is a rigid and laborious exam that encompasses all classes taken during primary school. Most students who long to continue their education begin the studying process six months or more before the exam. No doubt, to most students, the testing day could be the most important day of their lives, a day that determines if there is still a chance to better their lives and have a single opportunity to claim victory for one battle in a war that for most cannot be won. But the chances to succeed are almost insulting. Thousands of students apply for the exam every year, but only a few hundred make it. Of these few hundred, some earn their way in by merit, while others pay their way in. In a place where corruption is rooted at its foundation, where corruption touches everything and everyone, an inhumane disequilibrium delivers an unfair and crooked model. I grew up in a place where corruption has been normalized, expected, and even worse, accepted and embraced. It was a fact that all the rich kids would be able to attend school regardless of their efforts or intellectual capabilities.

It was the spring of the midnineties. I was one of the thousands of students who applied for an opportunity to further my education. As of sixth grade, I had been an outstanding student, with some of the better grades in the school and even in the city. I had participated in academic, poetry, and art events. I had been the first ten-year-old to deliver a speech at the old baseball stadium as a reward for my writings on global issues. I stood in front of thousands of people, military generals, and even the city major. Most importantly, I stood in front of a proud and nervous mother who sat amid the loud crowd. I did not see her, but cognizant of my mother's corporal expressions under great stress, I knew that somewhere in the stands sat a proud woman who, in the intensity of the moment, rocked her body back and forth with her arms extended and rubbing the upper part of her legs. In this back-and-forth motion, her hands remained partially closed, and her fingers and nails gave the appearance of an angry wild feline's trying to hurt her legs through the thickness of the clothes that she was wearing on the day. "You are each a pearl on my pearl collar," my mother would always say to us, "one that I wear proudly every day. You all make me proud." On that day, my mother's imaginary pearl collar flashed like the stars and overwhelmed her with joy and gratitude.

By the spring of the midnineties, I had accomplished many academic and athletic goals. I was a disciplined, driven child with a flattering competitive spirit. However, life at home was dark and on edge. There were many nights when I saw my mother rock back and forth at the edge of the bed with her head defiantly and frantically disrespecting the rhythm of her body. I could have sworn that her head wanted to leave her body. Her mouth was half-open and her cheeks weary as the soft moonlight filtered through the pores of our old curtains and revealed the tears on her unsettled face. Her mute cry gave the appearance of a drowning body that struggled to breathe, and her hands appeared to be chained loosely to her thighs. Why did I not hug her? Instead, I pretended to sleep even when my body was the furthest from resting.

Each second, each minute delivered us closer to my father's arrival, when all chaos would break loose. The outcome was always unpredictable. On this particular night, my father arrived drunk and volatile in character as always. Our one-bedroom cinder-block house with metal doors was no match for my father's wrath. As the five of us slept on the same full-size bed and kept our bodies warm under the multiple blankets, we heard him enter the house. Perhaps he was trying to make a statement or impose fear. Perhaps he was just drunk and unstable, but the slamming of the door sounded like thunder. It was almost like he wanted to detach the doors' welded hinges. The loud sound woke everyone rapidly, but my mother and I had already been expecting his arrival. It was clear now that it was going to be a long night. He stood by the door, catching his balance as he composed his legs first, then his shoulders. The smell of alcohol and cigarettes quickly extended through our small house, overtaking the smell of the cozy blankets. He then turned on the lights and lit every corner of our small house, including our small bedroom. For a fraction of a second, the child in me actually believed that the blankets over our heads blocking the sudden disrupting lights could protect us from my father. *If only the blankets could be our shield. If they could act as a wall that he could not trespass,* I thought.

But my silly thoughts were shattered as he deliberately slammed the kitchen table with the strength of lighting hitting the ground. It was a statement of fury and power. It was a declaration of war on five innocent and defenseless creatures and the official beginning of the conflict. My mother, wearing her motherhood armor, rapidly got out of bed and said with a fractured and hesitant voice, "The children are asleep, and I need to work tomorrow. Can you please go to sleep?" Perhaps it was the tone of her voice that made my father perceive as an order the soft statement—one that was uttered in the most humble and nonconfrontational way. Perhaps it did not matter what she could have said on that night; my father was drunk and ready to fight at all costs. My mother was not done speaking when he approached her violently, forcing his chest against hers as he pushed her against the wall. His arms, hanging on the side of his body, were tense and veiny, with his fists closed tightly. I was certain that in a split second, he would begin punching my mother in a relentless, bloody way. My mother, defenseless and overpowered, turned her head sideways, closed her eyes tightly, and with a great effort was able to pass her arms through the middle of their chests, not pushing him back or even trying to force him away but simply protecting her chest from his. As if my father thought he had lost some ground with her arms between them and he needed to recover it, he bent his head forward, pushing his forehead against my mother's cheeks with noticeable pressure. He looked like an enraged bull breathing heavily on my mother. His body looked tense and firm like solid rock. It was like he wanted to force my mother through that brick wall with his strength, but the wall refused to give in. A couple of seconds went by that felt like long minutes. My mother cried inconsolably against that wall, but even her cry was under attack. Her cheeks and mouth forced against that wall were unable to utter much noise as her lungs struggled to breathe.

The fast but aggressive scene completely awoke my siblings, who now cried frantically as well. My brother, who at the time was no more than six years old, had peed on our bed out of fear, and my sister shivered like she had just been rescued from frozen water. I, crying and lightly immune to the noise around me that I had grown accustomed to, ran to my father with a cry for mercy. With all the strength of my body, I hugged his leg, asking him to stop. My tears and the drooling of my mouth wet his dirty jeans as I begged for mercy, for him to leave us alone. It took him only a small effort to get rid of me and kick me away, but then, on this particular night, he stopped. Without saying a word, he stepped back and took one step toward the door. If only my mother would have remained against that wall for a few seconds, he might have left in peace and not come back until later or even the next day. However, my mother, aware of the needs at our house and with a reasonable but hesitant tone, said as he was walking away, "Could you please not take the car with you? I need to work tomorrow and need to drive the kids to school. I do not want to walk with them in the cold weather." A second did not pass after my mother had finished her sentence when my father turned around with lighting speed and fully extended his arms in a forceful, fast motion like a sucker punch, pushing my mother away. The impact was so strong that my mother's full body went flying a few feet back, landing on her back and hitting the back of her head.

Anger is an intriguing feeling that has the ability to blind humans no matter their age. The anger of a kid whose toy just got taken away and the anger of an adult who was done wrong by another person, in a way, are the exact same feeling. What makes anger look different, be different, is the maturity and self-control with which one handles it. Besides, in the event that anger is released and set free to destroy the thing or person which one's anger is directed to, the level of damage that one can make is limited by the resources that one has at hand to create that damage, to hurt or destroy that person or thing.

The anger that I felt on that night when I saw my father hurt my mother awoke an unexplored side of me. It was a side that until that night had been timid and defenseless. It was too fragile and undetermined, but it was not anymore. In that second, my fear had turned into pure hate, and the world had gone mute around me. I did not feel anymore; I did not measure consequences anymore. There was not a reason, only a goal: to hurt him. I saw nothing but him, the creator of this anger, of this energy within me that was bigger than myself but did not scare me. Like a predatory animal that attacks its prey unannounced out of the darkness and transforms a safe moment into death, I unleashed the strength that I did not have as a young boy and rushed against my tumbling, drunken father with every part of my body. Until this day I don't know if he even felt me hitting his body, but in this chaotic scene, he managed to get in the car and leave. That did not stop me. At that point there was more to hurt and destroy, so I grabbed all rocks around me because they had been placed there for my purpose, and I threw them at that old noisy car as he left. When my throw could not reach him anymore, I ran after the car as I continued to throw rocks and screamed vulgarities that had never been uttered out of my innocent mouth. And as I ran, the car slowly got smaller with the distance and my anger began to evaporate. It was like the effort of the running and my agitated lungs cleansed my head and my heart and returned my vision, and I was that innocent boy again. I headed back home to tend to my mother and siblings. My father did not return for another year. My siblings, my mother, and I went back to our normal lives the next day and, as always, wore our discreet masks, hiding the violence of our world from everyone. The next morning, the world could have sworn that we went to bed under a nighttime story followed by dreams about superheroes and princes.

I still remember my sweaty palms pressing and rubbing on that number 2 pencil as the proctor passed along the exams facedown on our desks. The day of the admittance exam was here, and there was no mercy for those who were not ready. The few hours of sleep I had the night before after processing what had happened did not matter. All was already stored in that area of my memory that I constantly fought to forget. It was a day to determine my future. My mother and I had agreed that I would test for the best school in town. It was a school known for having many affluent students whose parents were rich in town. That statistic alone limited the number of students who would be accepted based on merit versus economic status. However, it was the best opportunity I had at receiving a good education. For this reason, my mother spent long hours going over school materials with me. My preparation for this exam had not started a few weeks or months before. My mother had prepared me all my life.

My childhood's playtime had always been contingent upon finishing my homework. My mother had always been the mean mother on my whole block, the only one who would not allow me to play soccer until the homework and studying was done. I sat in that old wooden table for hours and hours while my ears were tortured with the sound of the other kids playing soccer on the street along with my mother's annoying and heartless commandments: "You cannot go outside until homework is done and you help me clean all your stuff." Her will to prepare me in life and to teach me the value of education went as far as becoming my teacher in fifth and sixth grade. Yes, my mother was my teacher, and while some may think this was convenient for me, those years were pure academic torture. Never after those two years did I ever have a stricter teacher in my life or the biggest pressure on my shoulders to do well in my education. "For the grace of God, you were born to be the head and not the tail," she never got tired of repeating to us, "but you will have to work hard for it because this world does not owe you single thing."

The exams lay facedown on our desks, and a painful silence amplified the sound of our heavy breathing. My heart beat fast. "You MAY START NOW!" the proctor shouted. His face was like the face of a skeptical law officer who assumes you are guilty of the crime. His pupils moved faster than his head in a scanning motion left to right. In his mind, we were all there to cheat, and his goal was to catch us doing it. He did not even allow himself to blink, as for that split second, someone may do something criminal. He was there to stop us. No, he was born to stop us. That was his only mission in life. I did not care for him, and with a mix of confidence, extreme nervousness, and a nauseous feeling, the tip of my number 2 touched the exam for the first time to write my name first, then the date. Then, I did not read the first question or the lengthy instructions explaining the complicated process of simply answering all the questions. Instead, I wrote across the top many initials separated by dots: "E.E.N.D.J.T.P .E.C.M.S.E.E.E.T.M.R.P.M.P.P.M.A." It was a prayer, and each of those initials were the beginning of a word. I prayed to God that He help me pass this test, and I put it in writing. I gave Him my stress and my worries. I knew that I needed to not only pass but to excel in order to be accepted. I knew I could not do it alone. I was not alone. The school had no choice but to accept the top students, as it would be these students who would continue to carry the academic integrity of the school and not those who paid their way in.

The results arrived a couple of weeks later. The school gates had opened, and the names of three hundred students were posted on a wall by the entrance on a small mural protected by glass doors. The grand rebar gates that were welded to the thick concrete pillars could have been similar to my idea of what heaven's gates looked like. They were tall and overly exaggerated in their design, with multiple twirls and spikes on top. It appeared like they had been built to impress and on an unlimited budget, mainly to stop all those who would dare to steal the education given within. I walked through the gates and saw myself on the shiny and polished concrete floors. I heard laughs and reassuring words. I heard crying and screaming. I also heard silence and the loud sound of high heels leaving the school saying more than the sound of their impact with the floor. They were conveying emotions—emotions that I choose not to see as I kept my face down, avoiding eye contact with anyone until I stood in front of the mural. At that point, all my senses were paused to aid the one that needed the most attention, my vision. My heart beat faster than my pupils could read through the long list of names. Skeptical of my placement, I began at 300 and thought about the 301st student. I thought about how the difference of one number had the power to change one's destiny. I thought that I could be 301. But there was no time to think. I kept going. I then arrived at 200 without seeing my name, and my nausea began. I was then at 100, and I really began to plan for the worst. Low in confidence and patience, I skipped to the top of the list and began to work my way down instead. It did not take long. My name was there—I was number 11.

It was a great blessing to do well on that test and to have the opportunity to further my education. By that point in my life, the preparation had been long and diverse. It had been a broad education, including the common subjects like history, math, and all academic-related topics. But it had also incorporated life subjects: obedience, morals, values, humility, faith, fear, failure, love, hard work, and most importantly, survival. In this last one, I had learned a variety of skills necessary to go through the long scary nights waiting for my father. It was things I could control, like sleeping with clothes and shoes and always ready to run. Keeping a knife under my pillow, reinforcing the door with furniture, sleeping away from the iron-guarded windows and always being ready to scream and fight. Under things I could control, I also learned to look for ways to make money in an honest way even as a kid. I learned to hide my emotions every morning and go through life like our nights did not happen. I learned to hide our clothes and anything of value that my father could sell for his addictions. By the time I finished elementary school, my mother, my siblings, and I had learned a second language—a sign language that allowed us to communicate with each other while my father was in the house. The reality was that there were more things that I could not control than what I could control. For instance, I could not control my fear of my father. I could not control the feeling of sinking on the bed, my accelerated heartbeat that suffocated my breathing, the uncontrollable shaking, and the imminent action of peeing my pants. I could not control anything that my father would do or his addictions, the stealing, the verbal and physical violence. The result of this lifestyle yielded a shy, quiet, and confused teenager. I was an inexplicable combination of talents, fears, sadness, life knowledge, disappointments, faith, dreams, and much, much anger.

CHAPTER 4

Born to Teach

THE SOUND OF the bell at one o'clock sharp was imminent. The bell would mark the end of the first school shift and the countdown to 1:45 p.m., which would be the beginning of the second shift. With so many kids and the lack of enough schools in the city, it was only prudent and necessary to create second shifts and even third shifts for some schools. Fifty to sixty students per class were more than enough for one teacher, and the learning was almost sporadic given the high numbers of students per class. Even though the alarm was activated manually by the school's principal, one could swear that it was activated by an automatic timer given how precise it was each and every day. Now that I think about it, I do not blame them for being so timely. The bell was not only the end of the shift, but the sound of freedom and the end of another long, exhausting day.

The loud bell would also trigger chaos. Almost like sprinters waiting for the sound of the gun or water being held back by the gates of a dam, hundreds of children and their teachers exploded out of their classrooms. Between the children, the teachers, the outdoor chip and soda vendors, and the parents in search of their kids, metaphorically speaking, I can only think of an anthill. Hundreds of future dreamers, some happy, most hungry, some fighting, most running, some lost, some found, spilling out—all this taking place under a single-color wave of blue-and-white uniforms. All schools required a uniform, which I now think of as a blessing as I can only wonder how many kids, including myself, would have had to wear a uniform of our own every day. I speak for the only couple of shirts and pants that I owned, and I am positive that others had less.

All but one classroom's door was affected by the punctual bell: my mother's. My mother was an elementary teacher, a woman born to teach; and luckily, she was able to pursue this career. The third one to be born out of nine siblings and the only one to complete an education as a result of God's blessings and both her and her mother's efforts. The family always tells the stories about my mother riling up the block at a very young age and playing "little school." She would work hard at creating choreographies where all the kids had to dance, sing, or write and present poetry. The whole thing went as far as some of the parents gathering on the street to see their kids act. The music bit would be unpredictable, played on an old record player with the one and only record they had, skipping through some sections, and pausing and accelerating through others. But an unstoppable music bit was not a concern as the laughs and screams were the real music. Instead, they were all thankful for the electricity now running through the street block. Early in my mother's life, it was an unforeseeable dream to have electricity flowing through the streets of this small Mexican city. Electricity was so far out of reach—so far that one of my mom's best memories of my grandfather was when he showed his kids the miracle of a light bulb, which at the time was only powered by the battery of their run-down 1950 Chevy.

At sixteen, my mother was able to apply to a federally subsidized teacher's school where the major obstacle was the number of students testing to get in. Yes, I said it, a subsidized school by the government. It was one of the few positive incentives the government subsidized for its people. There was no other way for my mom to receive an education. But with thousands of students testing and only a couple of hundred being accepted, the task could only be left to faith and a miraculous studying effort. There was no compelling entrance letter to the counsel needed, no need to push the tears out of some school official with the intention of softening his or her heart—you either got one of the greatest scores or did not.

Without a plan to fall back on or any other options available, the results finally came in, and my mother had made the list. The blessing of a stable job and income through my mother's career was the strongest pillar in our lives. The money was not much but consistent, so we were able to get by. In the midst of all struggles, my mother always reminded us of a worse scenario, where her childhood was usually the point of reference. Nevertheless, the struggles of a single mother of four with an alcoholic and drug-addicted husband were often hard to surpass.

Feeding four mouths was my mother's daily reminder of the power of God. Feeding nine, like her father and mother did, comforted her and gave her hope that pushing through life was possible in spite all its challenges. As a child with the awareness of an adult, my mother, hiding her petite body behind the empty, stained metal pantry, witnessed many cigarettes turn to ashes in my grandmother's dry lips as she sat on the kitchen table wondering about the origin of their next meals.

My mother grew up with many siblings, but the abundance of bodies alleviated some of the daily chores. Bringing water from the city well, for instance, became the duty of all siblings. The bigger the body, the bigger the container. My mother remembers the long line to fill up the kitchen pan she was assigned to and the long walk home balancing the container to retain each drop of water inside. Each drop of those containers then translated into showers, cooking, and drinking water. Each kid would pour as much as they could carry into the family welfare.

I should also talk a little bit about my *abuelo,* or my grandfather, a hardworking man with pragmatic solutions and a very strict father. Shoes for all his children, for instance, were never a matter of size. My mom and her siblings laugh at the memories of my grandfather cutting the tips of the shoes open, allowing them to wear these for a longer time. It was almost like making each shoe into a sandal. There was also the time when he dug their first septic hole in the backyard. The abundance of help of all ages and sizes was fruitful for this project as well. Each kid took a turn to get dropped into the hole with a rope my grandfather would pull in and out. With each trip, each child would take dirt out of the hole to dig it deeper and deeper. One full day of work, and a pack of dirty children, was a great reason for a shower in the cold oval steel bathtub. But the day could not end without a tasty meal. Beans and potatoes on the menu, marked the end of another blessed family day.

At nineteen, my mother met my father during a trip to the market. My mother and my *abuela*, or my grandmother, were both walking home as a shiny red car approached them. The driver rolled down the windows and asked if they needed a ride, to which my grandmother immediately refused. The driver of the car was my father.

"Can I then take you out sometime?" he asked my mom.

"I will need to ask my dad," said my mom shyly.

"I can ask him personally," he replied.

"Shouldn't you introduce yourself properly, young gentleman?" my grandmother questioned.

And so he did as he followed them slowly at walking pace all the way until they reached their house.

My grandfather was a rough man, so my father was lucky to not find him home on this day, and even luckier, my dad was able to convince my grandmother to let my mom go out with him the following weekend. A couple of hours of conversation in the summer night and a juicy burger from the neighbor's food stand was the body of their first date.

It only took a couple of dates before my dad proposed to my mom, mainly because they held a long-distance relationship and did not have much time in person together. My dad would jump between the United States and Mexico, and my mother would wait for him faithfully. Don't ask me how you go on two dates and decide to get married. "But those were different times," my mom would say every time I would ask. "Even though your dad and I are the same age, I was too innocent back then, son."

During the months that my father was away, my mom would also travel. My grandmother suffered from a rare disease, and she was forced to spend months in the capital of Mexico, which was about fifteen hours from home. My mother would travel with her as the hospital would host her as a guest as the treatment was being administered. My grandfather's job would pay for the cost of the medical bills, so that alone was a great blessing.

With a wedding around the corner and everyone in the town on the guest list, my mother, father, and grandmother traveled to the capital of our state in search of a wedding dress. After a dream day shopping for wedding dresses in the city, my mother bought a perfect, beautiful, classy dress with a long train, and as they were ready to leave the city, they were struck by a massive commercial train.

They called it the hill of the dead, and some just referred to it as the blind hill. My parents' accident was not the first nor the last that took place here. Their accident was not unique. There had been many casualties at this location—so many that there were stories about lost souls rummaging around as ghosts at night. I will stay away from ghost stories and tell you the truth about this place. Engineering at its worst, in combination with city officials who would much rather pocket the money than protect their citizens, led to many unnecessary deaths. The hill consisted of a dangerous incline followed by a bridge that had a rapid and short descent onto the train tracks, all made worse by large buildings obstructing the view of the train tracks. As you are reading, you are probably thinking about the train's horn or the train track guard rails, and the emergency lights. There were none. Also, bothering to pull the horn at each intersection was a regulation that most conductors took as a suggestion, not an enforceable protocol.

My dad, who was driving his truck, stepped on those brakes as hard as he could with the same intensity that my mom and grandmother screamed, while they too pushed on imaginary brakes under their feet, as if pressing hard against that dirty carpet would help the truck stop faster. The train dragged the vehicle to a near light post, where the truck got stuck taking the impact of each merciless train car one after the other until the end was reached.

Most commercial trains would pull about eighty cars. Eighty impacts. Each of those bringing their lives closer to an end. Miraculously, they all survived the accident with non-life-threatening injuries.

However, my grandmother became very sick as she continued to fight this strange disease, and with less than a month before the wedding, my grandmother made a promise to my mom to be out of the hospital by her wedding day.

In a traditional wedding, the groom does not get to see the bride until the magical walk down the aisle. This is the final moment before the "I do." For my mother, her wedding also started by walking down an aisle. Except this aisle was not the typical ribbon- and flower-decorated version with everyone looking their best, flashing enormous white smiles. Instead, my mother walked down the hospital aisle that led to my grandmother's room, where all her siblings waited impatiently for the doctor to deliver good news. All dressed up for the wedding and crying so hard they were gasping for breath, they learned that my grandparents had lied all this time. It turned out that there was no such thing as a strange disease, but instead only metastatic cancer. The truth had been hidden from my mother and siblings for years, but with my grandmother's condition rapidly deteriorating, it was only prudent to inform the family, even on the wedding day.

My grandmother had been transported to a local hospital from the capital, for the purpose of being in our town for the day of the wedding while still receiving her health care. But the trip to our town only made her condition worse, and she almost died that night. Have you ever heard of the expression "The show must go on"? My grandmother grabbed my mother by the cheeks with her weak, pale hands and pulled her close, and as she gently removed a mix of tears and makeup from my mother's disappointed eyes, with a feeble whisper, she begged my mother to continue with the wedding. There were no memories of laughter or joy the day after the wedding. No hurting feet from dancing. Not even a hangover. To this day, I have never seen my mother have a single drink of alcohol. My mother cried until there were no more tears.

She walked that hospital aisle to find out that my grandmother had only a few days left to live. A few minutes after, she then walked the dream wedding aisle in sad tears perfectly camouflaged as the tears of a joyful bride. Twenty-eight days later, my grandmother joined God in heaven after a long secret fight with cancer. A week after her death, my mother learned that she was pregnant with her first child, me.

CHAPTER 5

Crossing Paths

CORN TORTILLAS IN Mexico are the glue that put together all meals. Tortillas are more than a complement to a meal in Mexico; they are the foundation to every breakfast, lunch, and dinner. Tortilla stores, *tortillerias*, are a piece of everyone's daily routine, cooking thousands of tortillas daily. I always enjoyed the smell of *tortillerias* and marveled at the rotating band coming out of the oven delivering thousands of fresh steaming tortillas per hour. The secret to a perfect tortilla, aside from the ingredients, is the temperature at which it is served. Personal preference of temperature will always come into the equation, but for the most part, a freshly made corn tortilla should be served warm. On the opposite side of the perfect flavor and tortilla texture, we find a cold tortilla. Freshly made corn tortillas in Mexico do not have preservatives. Therefore, when they lose their warmth and get cold, they also lose their flavor and get hard or chewy. The great majority of people in Mexico would not approve the taste and texture of a cold corn tortilla by choice. To put it in perspective, even in poverty, I remember my mother giving cold tortillas away to the dogs on the street. She would rather see the food fill the dogs' bellies than be thrown away. In my house, throwing food away was not ever an option. "Wasting food is a major sin," my mother would tell us every day.

The choice of tortilla temperature was not an option to my mother in her childhood, and neither was the one and only option on the daily school lunch menu, cold corn tortillas with beans. My mother's only choice each day was whether to chew on those cracked, cold tortillas with dry beans or walk home hungry. In our city, school lunch was never provided so kids could either bring money or lunch. My grandmother, who faced the task of sending six out of the nine children to school with lunch, happily made the only affordable menu option by packing bean tacos for everyone. Yes, it was poor people's food but nevertheless packed with love.

It was during a normal day of school in my mother's freshman year in high school that she and my dad made contact for the first time. I know that I previously explained that they met on a trip to the market, but life had crossed their paths at an early age in school.

My father was born in a town right next to my mother's. A very small, old, colonial, Catholic town built when the agricultural and mining industries were booming at the end of the revolution. Among other factors, like its many churches built to impress the human eye and their saints, the town became famous for the huge soda plant at its heart. Nevertheless, even with signs of industrialization, the small religious town that saw the birth of my father remained untraced on most maps.

My father was the youngest of all siblings, the thirteenth. Some people believe the number thirteen is synonymous with bad luck. Others go as far as to avoid important dates that fall on this number like weddings and important life events. It is not uncommon to find buildings that skip the thirteenth floor for matters of superstition. However, my father—a superstitious man born as the thirteenth child—was far from being born out of luck.

A spoiled human being right out of the womb, my father was a miracle baby born when my grandmother was fifty years old. By the time my father was born, his siblings were already edging their thirties and living well-established lives. In this unique setup, he was born into a pampered life. My father, unlike my mother, grew up in better economic circumstances than my mother. His father, my grandfather, was first a miner who saved enough money to then become a wealthy land and cattle owner. By the time my father was born, he already built a stable life and saved a lot of money.

At his school, everyone knew my father as the chubby kid with many friends. At a time and in a place when having additional pounds on one's body was not a sign of an irresponsible lifestyle but the sign of wealth, my father was the poster child. Lunch breaks at school, also known as soccer time, delivered a herd of thirsty, dusty, and sweaty kids looking to cool down their bodies. Money, even at a young age, can buy most people friends. My father, whose pockets were always full of cash, made it a habit to buy soda for all kids who surrounded him. Needless to say that the option between drinking water from the one and only rusty faucet at school or cold soda from the little store was very clear; my father was an artificially loved child.

It was during one of those days when my father was approaching the little school store, surrounded by thirsty kids, that his and my mother's eyes made contact for a split second for the very first time. That moment drastically depicted two different realities. My mother biting on that cold tortilla awaiting a drink from the faucet so that she could swallow the dry beans as my father prepared to feed his ego by buying every fake friend a soda. It is sad to say that even the kids lined up for a drink of the rusty water faucet were more of a friend to my mother than the herd of sweaty kids drinking free soda were to my father. At least, at the line for a drink of water, all kids shared the same thirst, the same scarcity. Some filled their bellies with water for lunch, while some, like my mother, who were a bit richer among the poor, impatiently waited to aid her saliva in the fight to digest her cold lunch.

Life is funny and unpredictable in nature. Who would have been able to foresee that the near future would bring them together? Even then, as kids, eye contact between my parents meant nothing. Their lives did not have anything in common, and while they shared the same school and teachers, they were both strange to each other on this day and remained this way for all their lives.

My mother grew up humble and appreciative of every meal, every laugh, and every drop of warm water. My father grew up entitled and egocentric. His childhood was unchallenging, and his life perspective became disoriented and unfounded.

Growing up well-nourished and the furthest away from poverty is a great blessing. The problem was that my father's childhood was built around effortless gratification. This upbringing was responsible for creating an adult who lacked accountability or any sense of responsibility for his actions. My father lacked resilience and life-battling endurance. There were no battles in his childhood that weren't fought for him. There was never the taste of an earned victory or an accomplishment at any level, and in his mind, everything he had he was already entitled to.

As much of an irritable macho man as my grandfather was, my father grew up without a true authority figure. My grandfather, old and tired after twelve children, gave my father, the thirteenth child, his softer and tired side. On the maternal side, my grandmother was an angel. She was a loving woman who lived for her children. Her mistake was to offer my father her unconditional sympathy regardless of his actions. Unable to say no to him, she always stood by his side excusing his behavior. My father never got tired of taking advantage of her. Her love for her youngest son was blind and unable to see his mistakes to the point that it hurt him. For our love to be constructive for our children, we must concurrently love and offer discipline, structure, and accountability.

Contrary to my father's profile of entitlement, something in him, which I am unable to describe, made him a hardworking man when his will to do so allowed him to work. Almost out of the ordinary, a spark of the man he could have been with the right upbringing and the right values, my father could stand out from the crowds with his ability to push hard. He could build an impeccable reputation of hard work in days, even hours, but just as fast as he would build it, he would destroy it. He lacked the mental toughness and patience to keep a job. I cannot excuse my father for his actions, but I know for certain that his childhood was the foundation for his behavior.

* * *

My children, when we are young, it is easy to confuse our parent's disciplinary actions with something other than love. As a child,

I thought of my mother as unfair and antiquated many times. But now life has taught me that her rules and discipline were founded in love and, most importantly, in the word of God. My mother always made it clear that God would always be willing to forgive us, but we would always be responsible for the consequences of our actions. Her words never left me alone even when I wished for her teaching to go away. Her words, God teachings, hunted me down and stayed by my side. Let the lessons I have taught you and my writing in this book all together compel your heart and your mind. And make no mistake, I love you more than any words will ever have the ability to articulate.

* * *

At age sixteen, my father moved to live with one of his sisters in the United States. While he did not stay permanently, he made it a routine to travel back and forth, staying a few months each trip. During his time in the United States, he held labor jobs that allowed him to save money. Money that he would then go back to Mexico with and spend on luxuries, friends, and his number one habit, drinking.

In the United States, he also lacked an authority figure, gaining even more freedom. His sisters would provide him with shelter, food, and most of the essentials. It was at some point during one of those trips to the United States that he began using drugs and drinking heavily. Without the need to save money or do anything constructive, he lived a chaotic and unhealthy life. Going out to bars and frequent nights out, he lived life at large, full of empty, materialistic pleasures like driving fancy cars and wearing expensive clothes.

My father's addictions, for the most part, did not get in the way of his looks. During his twenties, my father always maintained a clean-cut look, always worried about appearing his best. His clean looks allowed him to deceive people and ultimately woo my mother to marry him. I still cannot comprehend what made him want to get married. Perhaps he saw my beautiful mother as a trophy, one that he acquired easily and wanted to make his own. Maybe my mother met my father during a good stretch in his life where he was able to control his addictions and inject some wisdom into his reckless life.

A couple of days after my parents' wedding, at a time when my mother needed his undivided support as my grandmother was dying, my father did not come home for the night. My mother, extremely worried, looked for him, thinking that something bad had happened. However, she was confused and astonished when she found him by the river, drinking with friends, happy and euphoric. As she approached him, he turned aggressive and even jealous as his drunk friends made advances on her. It only took three dates and two days of marriage for my mother to learn the truth about him and have her already sad heart broken.

Most newlyweds cannot get enough of each other. The first days of marriage are almost magical. But for my mother, life was not exactly a fairy tale. It was on that day, between the sound of the river and my father yelling, demanding she go back home, that my mother's real journey with my father began.

Why did my mother stay with him? I often wonder.

"I don't regret anything," my mother would always tell me and my siblings, followed by the story of the day when she found herself questioning God for all the battles that she had to fight. She fought economic and spiritual battles, and often she pled to God for help or even a sign that He was there for us. My mother would ask for the smallest sign that would prove that God was watching, that He had a plan for us and that life would change one day at the sound of His mighty command. She felt so lonely. "It's almost like I could hear his voice talking to me," she said to us, "'Have you not seen the blessing I have given you through your children?'" It was on that day that my mother understood that God was in control despite the situation. It was her blessing and responsibility to raise us in His word and will. No matter the drought, no matter the scarcity, He had a plan; He was in control.

CHAPTER 6

Transformation

THE SMELL OF eggs and onions traveled through the desk rows of our class of about fifty students every morning. The smell was so strong that the whole class could notice it. It was an invasion of the classroom already overwhelmed with the smell of paper, chalk, and students. But the smell did not make anyone hungry. Instead, it was the first bullying event of the day or sometimes the second or third. The events were many, and the reasons even more. One morning it could have been my cheap knockoff shoes named Nikx with an identical swoosh or the silver dental crown wrapping my dead, dark front tooth. In the absence of any reasons, the rich kids were creative enough to find ways to bully me. I did not belong in their close circle or social class. I was simply a nerdy-looking kid with a bull's eye on my forehead. Even with the experience I had gathered at this point in my life, I was fragile and innocent, always running away from conflict. The rich kids at school were almost like an organized mafia—one that only those with an affluent status could enter. They were entitled and poisonous. They did not take orders; they did not need guidance. They were the owners of every classroom and most teachers. They set the cadence of every class. They were untouchable, arrogant, and pampered. Life had never tested them nor hurt them. They controlled life like a producer controls the filming of a movie. They were there to film their own movie. The learning was not necessary. There were no battles in their future nor races or challenges.

They were already the winners, the owners of it all, and everything around them was simply there to serve them because their presence alone was holy.

Because there was no way on earth that I could afford to buy lunch at school, my mother would pack my lunch every day. Most of the time my lunch consisted of an egg sandwich cooked with multiple vegetables, including onions. The sandwich itself always tasted delicious, but the action of carrying the sandwich in my backpack was the main issue. Even when I would wrap my lunch in multiple plastic bags, the smell of it was unstoppable. Every morning, the action of pulling one of my notebooks from my backpack would unleash the smell of sulfur to the entire classroom. Rich kids reminded me every morning of how much the smell bothered them with spits and head whacking as the teachers wrote on their chalkboards. I thought about solutions, like not bringing lunch to school or burying my sandwich in the garden. The first one would starve me, and the second one would be an easy find for the dogs or cats, so I did my best at enduring the torture for not being able to afford the delicious sandwiches that they would sell at school. The number of times that I stopped by the school cafeteria in my three years at this school were few. I simply did not carry any money with me ever. Instead, I picked the back of a classroom building at the furthest south point of the school. That was my favorite place. It was a hidden little corner facing the main street. Sitting on the ground with my back against the block walls of the building, I could see all cars driving by on the street through the rusted wire fence. At a distance, I could hear the loud crowd of kids, but the noise was interrupted by the old cars and motorcycles driving by.

There were many local buses with their smoky pipes and their loud clutches. There were people walking by who at times would make eye contact while others pedaled slowly on their tired-looking bicycles.

While I muscled through the many bags that wrapped my sandwich and uncovered the now-soggy bread and cold eggs, I dwelled on the memories of previous nights and the stress of my homework.

There were also times when I fantasized about the day when my karate moves would defend me from the rich kids. I saw myself taking on the entire clan with Bruce Lee moves in an epic fight. Of course, all this would happen in the presence of the prettiest girl at school who would look at me and admire me for my agility and strength. Such courage would be compensated with a kiss. But I had never kissed a girl before. I would not know how to do it. Even while daydreaming, I would panic about my first kiss. Then, my daydreaming was often interrupted with a violent need to drink something to pass that sandwich through my throat. Snapping out of it and coming back to reality, I would walk to the nearest water fountain and drink slowly to not feel pain while the food made its way down to my stomach.

Maybe the karate moves would have saved me from the countless nicknames I was given as the result of my silver-crown front tooth. At age ten, I had fallen while running on a brick sidewalk, breaking my front tooth and leaving it looking like a perfect triangle. Such a perfect trigonometric figure was not the main problem but the many nerves that were damaged. The terrible pain after I had broken my tooth was unbearable. My mother, with very limited resources, was forced to take me to a dentist who accepted to fix it on a low-payment plan. Most people would get their tooth fixed with porcelain or available materials that would take care of the aesthetics of their smiles. That was not an option for me, and with our low budget, we were only able to afford a shiny silver crown around the already dead tooth that eventually turned black. Such a needed fix to my tooth was weaponized by the rich kids at school through insults and infinite reasons to mock me. But it was not only the bullies at school. People struggled to make eye contact with me. I could see their eyes drawn toward my mouth as soon as I spoke or smiled. It was something hard to ignore even while one strenuously tried to do so. Such events in my life hid my smile for many years and damaged my confidence.

But not all people noticed the bad looks of my front tooth. Not all people noticed my inability to laugh freely at life and its unexpected jokes—the type of laugh that leaves your ribs and jaw sore, the laugh that would have replaced the tight-lipped, ear-to-ear smile pressing hard against my teeth so the shine of my silver tooth was not noticed. He was the son of a renowned dentist in town, and his family was very wealthy. However, he was not part of the school clan, nor had he been accepted into the school by paying his way in. His motives in life were different and, to many, unknown. He did not notice others as much as others noticed him occasionally. He walked through school like a ghost. His walking was slow and pre-determined. He walked like a man on a mission, yet he looked calm and often lost. His pants, usually shorter on the ankles, revealed the unmatched pair of socks he would always wear. He wore his shirts in ways that no one with a small sense of fashion would, always wrin-kled and short on his torso, revealing a section of his stomach and lower back. His face was always pale, and his eyes bright in perfect circular shapes. When he smiled, the tip of his lips seemed to touch his ears. His nose, long and sharp, was not shaped like that of any other kid in school, and perhaps it was the most distinguished part of his face. It was his nose that the clan tried to attack and make the center of ridicule, but their tactics never worked. Victor could not be bullied or be made fun of. He simply did not see or need others or cared for their opinions. Instead, he found fulfillment in his strange and progressive hobbies, which were unique for the time and place in which we were living, like video games and Asian cartoons. He also enjoyed art, specifically acting.

At first, I too was guilty of not noticing him. At age twelve, during the second week of classes in history class, we all heard a loud sneeze followed by, "Teacher, I sneezed so hard that my boogers came out, and now they are all over my book!" It was nearly impossible not to laugh after hearing the panic in Victor's voice and how con-cerned he was with the situation. But as the professor walked toward Victor to help him, he and I made eye contact for the first time, and surprisingly, I felt embarrassed. The split second when our sight crossed ways, I felt as if I had been the one sneezing too hard. I real-ized that making fun of him would turn me into the aggressor and not the victim I always was. This feeling troubled me greatly. In that split second, I also noticed his peace and ability to tune out everyone around him and not care. I found great comfort in his strength and felt immediately attached to him in a peculiar and proud way. I realize now and knew then as well that my empathy for him was, without a doubt, selfish. Deep inside, my motives for seeing him as my friend were egotistic. I could use him to protect my fears and strengthen my weaknesses or, at the very minimum, ignore them. I wanted to be like him, free and careless, in full peace with myself and detached from the malice of this world.

After that class, Victor and I became best friends. He never got tired of telling me that I was his best and only friend, and neither did I. We walked through school together, selected the same classes, and spent hours laughing about the silliest things and fantasizing about our futures. We discussed history and all the world wars. We argued about Don Quixote and his metaphors. We questioned the objectivism of math and physics and wondered if it was true that aliens gave us all the answers. Who built the pyramids? Was Darwin right about the origin of men? Who will enter puberty first? Should we shave our thin mustaches? I never became tired of his abnormal behavior and learned to enjoy his spontaneous reactions and my inability to read his decisions. He was a smart kid, a genius who required minimal studying to excel in school. There were many times when I pictured him in front of the class, teaching us all the complexities of math and the ironies of human history, but instead he drew cartoons and wrote theater plays in the back of the class and passed all his exams with As. Victor and I were both in theater class, although we both acted for different reasons. He was in it for the love of acting and his passion for arts. I was in it to detach myself from reality and assume the many roles I was given. I was in it because I wanted to be someone else from time to time, and he was in it because he wanted to bring his personality into each of the characters he played.

With our backs against that wall and facing the road in front of us during recess, I ate my egg sandwich while he ate the expensive sandwiches from the cafeteria. He never once offered me a bite. I never asked him to or showed him any signs of wanting a piece of that delicious meal. Victor did not judge my life, nor did he have an idea of the issues I had a home. We never talked about it. He did not understand economic statuses outside of an economics class and textbook content. He also never found himself in the middle of violence and disparity. He never visited my house, but when spending time at his house, he had a computer, which at the time was nearly impossible to afford. I sat next to him for hours, marveling at the many uses of such a monitor and dreaming of the time I could afford one. He never noticed that he never let me use it as I never asked him to use it, nor did I give him any signs that I wanted to use it. I found peace in his lack of social skills or empathy for others. In Victor's world, there was neither sharing nor selfishness. The thought of selfishness alone would imply that the world was not there for him and him alone. The thought of sharing would imply that others lack or need something that can only be acknowledged or noticed if you pay attention to others. Victor was alone in his mind. Yet at the center of this genius kid with poor social skills and awkward dressing choices, there was a humble soul that meant no harm to anyone. He had the ability to love me as a friend, never judge me, and simply be present in my life when I needed him most.

In our second year of school, as we began to turn into teenagers, we began to notice all the girls in school and dreamed of the day we would have our first girlfriend and our first kiss. We spent many afternoons plagiarizing poems from the most famous poets in history and making them our own. However, none of the letters we sent or personally delivered succeeded in getting us a girlfriend. Instead, the clan found reasons to make fun of both of us and deployed dirty tactics like hiding our backpacks or pushing us to the ground by surprise while we were attempting to deliver a love letter. Victor never complained, and I found peace in his lack of care for others. However, from time to time, he would speak about the day we would both join a kickboxing class and put each of those kids in their place. We never did.

During our first semester of the second year of school, the school board posted many flyers about the annual chess tournament, encouraging students to enroll. The intriguing pictures of a chessboard with its horses and pawns motivated me to enroll. Before the day of the tournament, I had never played chess in my life. My only memory of chess was from an old movie I had once watched where an old man said, "The man who does not play chess is not a man." I thought, *There must be something that I can learn from this game.* An hour before the tournament began, Victor, who had also enrolled, gave me a crash course on how to move the pieces and on the purpose of the game. As expected, I lost every single game and went home defeated. However, it was the beginning of a passion for a game that I was to play for the rest of my life. During the next annual tournament, I placed second, losing the final game but feeling like a winner. From there, I went on to play many other tournaments at school and throughout the state. More than a hobby, chess became a lifestyle—almost like an addiction. Sitting at home I could strategize plays on the tile of the bathroom. While walking in school, the plaza and its concrete squares on the floor were an opportunity to plan a move before the game. Most importantly, Victor and I found a game to spend our afternoons trash-talking each other about the massive destruction we were about to unleash on each other.

It was not long after understanding the game of chess that I learned that life itself is a combination of multiple chess games being played. In each game there is a king to kill and a strategy to deploy. There is a need to think ahead, to make sacrifices and to not waste any moves for the sake of taking a step. I viewed each king in each game as my dreams and goals. Chess reinforced the fact that every choice has a consequence and analyzing each decision in depth by thinking many moves ahead is an effective way to live, but only when our thoughts are rational and healthy. At that point in my life, it was healthy to think more than twice before acting. Chess helped me calm my mind and move through life with the best outcome as my goal, regardless of the circumstances that surrounded me. Each piece on the board, while with different strengths and skills, can be lethal. This fact was a great reminder that in life even small accomplishments matter and require hard work, patience, and determination.

* * *

Children, to the extent that you can, live your life with the thoughtfulness and premeditation of a chess game. Understand that every decision you make will carry long-term consequences. Think about the right sacrifices, that while those are the ones that hurt most, more often than not, they will deliver the most rewarding outcomes. Protect your king with passion and at all cost, where your king is your values, your morals, and most importantly, your faith. Make your king your goals, your dreams, and the unachievable. No matter the circumstances of the game, whether favorable or against you, respect your rival and remain humble. Never underestimate the consequences of one bad decision in life, which can easily turn the game against you. Give your all in each game, as playing with everything you have is part of showing respect for you rivals too. Expect each game to be the most difficult, and always be prepared to change your strategy and start all over with the many or few pieces you have left. One last thing: learn to lose. Be prepared to lose, because losing in life is always an option. I hereby make reference to a game of chess with its rules and its respectful handshake. However, life will not always follow the rules. Learn that even when you stay true to yourself and thoughtful about your every single move, the outcome will not always be positive. You will fail—you will fail even when the checkmate is close and you follow every single rule. Be prepared to dust off, to shake your failures off, learn from them, and go on with your life. There is far more wisdom earned in losing than in winning.

* * *

During my years at secondary school, life went by quickly. Between the fun I had with Victor, homework, home issues, and work, the day never seemed to have enough hours. However, life did not go fast enough to make me forget some of the struggles that my family and I endured. In the fall of ninth grade, I was able to get a job at a bakery, cleaning and helping with inventory. The smell of the freshly baked doughnuts was so overwhelming and delicious that it made the job comfortable, even when the owner never let me eat a single doughnut. From the big glass door, I could see the town market, which always had several vendors selling knockoff clothes and shoes. For a while now, I had been thinking about Student's Day, a day when all students at school were allowed to not wear a uniform. For most kids, the day could not come any sooner. For me, just to learn about the day coming would make me anxious. The first student day I spent at school, I ended up wearing an old set of shorts and shirt with what I believe was the drawing of a cartoon from a television show made for kids five and under. The mocking and laughing was so intense that I left school early and told my mother that they had made it a short day. The second year, I pretended that I forgot that I did not have to wear a uniform, which prompted the rich kids to make fun of me. The truth was that I did not have any decent clothes to wear to school, and a school uniform was my way to level the playing field superficially. The truth was that I had the same shirt and worn-out jeans that I would wear to church every Sunday and one good pair of shoes that I would wear to school every day.

With the third Student's Day approaching, from the glass door at the bakery, I kept staring at a pair of jeans for sale at one of the stores in the market. Saving all my money for three months would allow me to afford one pair that I could then wear to school with a shirt that my mother had bought me during the summer. The plan was in place, and it would work with plenty of sacrifice.

During the morning, I went to school; and during the afternoon, I went to work. I left my house early and came back late. I also worked Saturdays and half of Sundays. For three months, I did my homework wherever I could and rested whenever I could. This was not my first job, so it was not a big deal. The difference between this job and all others I had had by this age was the goal I had in mind, which selfishly, was not to help my family but instead to buy myself a pair of jeans.

In my memory, I see myself standing at the doughnut shop door, visualizing my goal: a knockoff pair of jeans that was always hung on a tight wire across the front of the stores, swaying with the wind. With each sway it felt like they teased me about coming my way and slipping away from my hands the very last second. Finally, a few months into the job, I was able to buy my jeans. They were dark blue, tight on the waist, and loose on the bottom, like the latest fashion trend. The brand must have been Levus or Levius. Clearly, the people who were making the pants did not have much of an imagination. But that did not matter, all I had to do now was be smart and wear a thick belt that would cover the fake brand tag and an untucked shirt.

When I arrived home, I showed my mother my new jeans, and she was happy for me. However, caring for me, she explained that the jeans needed to be washed before wearing them, "Just in case some dirty person tried them on," she said. "Also, you don't know how long they have been there for sale, accumulating dust. My kids are not going to wear dusty clothes." In a matter of a few minutes, my pants were hanging on a new wire, my mother's drying wire on the patio. In a matter of hours, we learned that washing the pants was a big mistake. With the wash, the dark-blue color faded away so drastically that it was hard to believe that my mother did not use bleach to wash them. The pants were now ruined. That's when my mind went quickly into problem-solving mode, but before I could think of a solution, my mother said, "Don't worry son! We can stain them back to normal. Go to the corner store, and buy a little bag of blue jean color stain"—this item was apparently a hot item I never heard about—"and we can fix them right away. You will be wearing new jeans to school tomorrow no matter what. That's an easy fix."

Hesitant but hopeful, I ran to the store and learned that there was a whole section of jean stain powder color at the end of the second aisle, next to the crazy glue and knee and elbow patches. We could have called it the "secondhand remedy kit aisle." Back at home my mother mixed the powder in water and submerged my jeans for some time until they were back to life with a solid-blue color. She then hung them on the wire again and promised they would be ready by the next morning.

The next morning, we woke up to a rainy street. I ran to the patio, praying that the pants were not too wet, but they were indeed soaked. I quickly spread the old white towel over my mother's bed and plugged in the iron to try to iron them dry. I was very gentle on the jeans, but even then I noticed the blue water coming out of them. It was getting late to go to school, so with the jeans semidry, I jumped on my bicycle and left. My long hours of work and preparation for the big day had paid off. I was on my way to my last Student's Day at secondary school with a brand-new pair of jeans, a nice shirt, and what I thought would be a bully-free day.

During Student's Day, we would always have fun activities and even lunch, so it was a day when I did not have to bring my egg sandwich. Everything was perfect. For the first activity of the day, we were asked to gather at the school patio, which was probably half the size of a soccer field with a concrete surface and where we would always gather every Monday morning to sing our national anthem. On this day, our school dean was to kick off the day with encouraging words about the future generations. He was a tall, skinny guy with a belly that belonged to someone three times his weight. He wore his hair too short, almost like military men did, and had an overgrown mustache. It was so long that his upper lip was never seen. Before he began speaking, he asked us to sit on the ground, which was never the norm as we always had to stand.

"Today, we are celebrating your day, so you can all sit right where you are," he said through the speakers hanging on the four light posts surrounding the patio. His mustache moved in all kinds of weird ways as he talked, and the one-second delay in transmission from the microphone to the speakers made it hard to take him seriously. "You are the future of this great nation. You are the future generations that…"

"Oh no!" I said to myself, panicking. I had forgotten my pants were wet, and after sitting on the hot, dry concrete ground, I would leave a blue stain on the ground after standing up. The next minutes after my realization sped up so fast that it felt like his usual and long boring speech had been too short.

"Now, go to your classroom and enjoy the day," he said. My heart raced so fast that I felt like I was in the middle of a workout. I stayed down for a few seconds, which felt like minutes, while most of the students stood up. I was thinking, *Maybe I can stand up fast and hide in the crowd. Maybe no one will notice if I wait until the end. Maybe I should stand up now so that no one can tell which pair of jeans left a blue stain on the ground.* In planning the logistics for a few seconds, I realized that I was in the middle of a wave of students walking in all directions, mirroring a stampede; I could not stay seated any longer, or I would risk being stepped on. I stood up slowly and took a forceful, quick peek at the ground, pretending everything was normal, and realized that my nightmare was true. There was a clear, well-defined, blue butt print on the pale-gray concrete ground, making it noticeable from any distance even among the dense crowd of students walking toward their classroom. What was worse was that the dry ground had sucked my jeans dry, and with it, the blue stain. Now the ground had a perfect blue butt print, and my jeans had a pale grey butt. It was so obvious it had been me that we did not need anything nearly close to Sherlock Holmes to put A and B together. The next minutes were so overwhelming that I don't remember much aside from multiple laughing faces pushing me from one side to another, I remember being kicked and a guy saying, "Look, he even stained my white shoes." My bike had never been pedaled so fast. I did not feel any fatigue or the bumps of the old semipaved streets. I wasn't only pedaling back home. As I pedaled, like a snake, I shed the harmless, peaceful, shy boy off me. I pedaled into another dimension, where my life was to change, *had* to change. I was stronger than them; I had lived more than them. They had no right to make me their clown! I had earned my stripes in a way that none of those kids ever had. I was the owner of my future. All that fear and suppressed anger poured out of me, giving me a new body. In the few miles that I pedaled back home, I transformed into a new being. I was now the result of a boiling pot of fears, anger, scarcity, sacrifices, uncertainty, abuse, and more. I had grown from boy to an angry teenager in a matter of miles.

The rest of the school year was a blink of an eye. I still brought my egg sandwich to school, played chess and laughed about the silliest things with Victor. I even got my first girlfriend, whom I kissed for the first time at a dark movie theater, which made me miss the end of the movie. Surprisingly, it only took one fight and a broken arm for the rich kids to leave Victor and me alone, although I am certain that it was the anger in my eyes with which I finally fought back and not the guy's broken arm that made them stay away from us. It had been a long and challenging three years of middle school. New adventures were to come as my journey was only beginning.

CHAPTER 7

Dreaming of America

SECONDARY SCHOOL IN Mexico is three years long and is the equivalent of seventh, eighth, and ninth grade in the United States. After secondary comes high school, which lasts for another three years. Like with secondary school, high school education is not a given right, and students must earn their way in through an exam. Also, like in secondary school, thousands of students apply and take the test, but only a few are accepted. There are fewer high schools than secondary schools, so the chances of attending high school are even slimmer. For many, finishing secondary school is their last intellectual accomplishment before joining the labor force full-time for the rest of their lives.

Similarly, with secondary schools, high schools came in all shapes and forms. There were academically outstanding schools and academically agonizing schools and everything in between. Social classes were well defined by schools, with the best options being in town with perks like nice architectural buildings and those on the outskirts of town on dirt roads and lacking the basic elements like potable water and air conditioning. There was also the monetary cost of going to good versus bad schools. The prominent schools in the city charged an insulting amount of money, not including the expensive uniforms and school supplies. It was not hard to predict which students would end up at which school, as everyone could be measured by their economic status. For example, the great majority

of students from the secondary school that I attended ended studying at the most expensive high schools. As I explained before, these
students and their families were entrenched in the city's bureaucracy,
including schools.

I did not think twice when my mother asked me what I wanted
to do. I knew I had high grades and had done well overall, so I could
easily test into one of the best schools in the city. However, I was
not willing to punish myself for another three years spending God
knows how many hours at school among such entitled and arrogant
students. The thought alone was preposterous and made me sick to
my stomach. "But, son, we can make a sacrifice and find a way to pay
for a good high school. I can ask for a loan or work a second shift,"
said my mother many times, trying to convince me to apply to one of
the best schools, but I affirmatively declined the offer every time. My
decision was not only based on how hard it was to survive secondary
school among such egotistical kids, it was more so about my mother
and the effort that she would have to make to pay for my school. My
sister had only a year left before she would start secondary school as
well, and my mother would need even more money—money that we
did not have.

After assessing my options, I decided to go to a middle-of-the-
road school located near the outskirts of town. The school was not in
perfect shape, but one could tell that there was pride in the way it was
taken care of. The first thing I noticed when I walked in was an old
guy wearing a dirty cowboy hat and pushing a broom slowly under
the harsh sun, trying to keep the concrete floors clean. However, all
it took was a little bit of wind to start the sweeping all over again.
Located on a dirt road, it was nearly impossible to keep the dust
off any surface. From a distance, the school and the old man with a
cowboy hat could have been part of a Western movie. The school had
a concrete basketball court with soccer goals and rusted basketball
rings that were once orange. Between two short rows of classrooms,
there was a big empty dirt lot that was used as a soccer field. The
ground on the lot was full of rocks and was the furthest away from a
flat surface, but it did the job. I also noticed that everything seemed
calm and peaceful. One could hear the broom sweeping the concrete

ground and creating a cloud of dust from a great distance. The school was small compared to my secondary school and did not have the grand entrance that my previous school had. Instead, two old metal doors with bad welding jobs hung from rusted posts that tiredly held a wavy and corroded wire fence. All the classrooms were built out of cinder block and had flat concrete roofs. There were trimmed bushes with asymmetrical shapes around most buildings and several recently planted short, thin trees. It took an amplified imagination to picture those trees tall and healthy many years ahead, but the man in the cowboy hat watered them slowly with poor water pressure from a long hose.

The day of the entrance exam arrived, and with great confidence, trusting in God that it was the right decision, I took it, placing top ten out of hundreds of students who applied. Victor, unfortunately, decided to go to the best and most expensive school in the city. We did not ask each other why we had made different choices, we simply promised to keep seeing each other and spending time together.

It was the beginning of a new journey. Life had given me an opportunity to start over. I even got a new look. I shaved my puberty mustache, which made my mother cry for a reason that I still don't understand. I also got my first haircut at a real barbershop, which made my mother cry again. Up until that day she had always cut my hair to save money. I walked the streets of our city with an overwhelming excitement. It was the beginning of a new season, and I felt fulfilled with the decisions that I had made to change my brand and my mindset.

On my first day of high school I met all my future classmates, who appeared to have so much in common with me. There was an air of peace and fun. Timely at eight o'clock, our first teacher arrived, sticking his head through the classroom's screenless window. He looked like he had been standing in the sun for a long time. His skin was so tan yet so dry that it looked like his cheeks were made out of paper. His hair was slicked back, revealing a well-defined widow's peak that gave away his age. He had a thick, dark mustache and a wide, shiny nose that did not match his dry face. He wore a confident smile and a shirt that fit him a little bit too tight for the size of his belly.

"Hello, guys," he said as his left hand pulled a cigarette box from his right-side shirt pocket. "Prepare to make friends that will last a lifetime and memories that will make you laugh forever. That is what high school will do to you." He lit a cigarette on the right side of his mouth and threw the empty cigarette box into a trash can near the window. "I am your political science teacher and we are going to have fun," he said as he squinted his eyes and took a deep hit of the cigarette. His whole class was casually taught from the window, him resting his body through it and adjusting his pants way too many times.

For our next class, a tall middle-aged guy walked into the classroom with a black briefcase and his head looking down as if he did not want to stumble over something on the floor. Judging by his hair, he had just gotten out of bed; judging by his wrinkly shirt, he did not care much for an iron. "I am your biology teacher. Let's go over the classroom rules." All I remember is that he used "no exceptions" and "unacceptable" too many times.

Next, there was our English teacher, who pretended to not speak Spanish. A short, skinny lady who wore her skirts too low, almost touching the ground. Her face was pale and long, with red lips and straight yellow teeth. She claimed to have lived in the United States—or at least that is what I understood from her introduction, which was done in English. At that time, English was the weakest of my classes, so I did not understand much.

On my first day of school, I met Noe. Noe was a tall skinny guy who looked eccentric at first glance. However, it was the type of eccentricity that makes a high school student look cool. His skin was darker than most of the other students and his eyebags well defined, as if he needed to sleep a lot more. He wore tighter clothes than all of us, which made his already big feet look even bigger. Even while we all had to wear a uniform, he always seemed to stand out from the class with his unique hairstyles or his choice of shoe fashion. He had a skinny face with a contagious smile. He always had the best jokes, but even while it made the whole class laugh, it did not hide the pain that I could see in his eyes. His teeth were stained severely, and he smoked like a chimney. He would always have a cigarette in his mouth even while eating lunch. His charisma and effort to hide an unknown source of pain gave him an extroverted personality that seemed to build a wall around his true emotions and secrets—secrets that I never learned about.

The first time Noe and I talked, he quizzed me about my music choices, which I failed greatly. By my first day of high school, all I had ever listened to was the 6:00 a.m. radio alarm that my mother used every morning to listen to the weather. There was not much diversity in the one and only available AM radio station available at home. Most songs were about broken love tales, the Mexican revolution, and the usual famous cartel stories. All came with the same traditional rhythm. I often wondered if it was all the same music but with different lyrics; even the singing voice sounded the same song after song. When I was twelve, one of my uncles had given me a radio as a Christmas present. I probably would have known more about music if I had kept it; however, the radio did not even make it to New Year's before my father stole it from me and sold it. I knew many Christmas carols and every church hymn ever written, but I did not know a thing about this music called rock. Noe explained that rock was the best music ever and that he would make me a cassette. "Just don't listen to people when they say rock is Satan's music," he said. "Their brains are too small to think outside of mariachi music." The next day, he brought me a cassette, which I played on my mother's school stereo that she had brought home for an activity that she was planning for her students. While I did not know much about music going into high school, I was certain that I did not like what everyone else was listening to. However, I did not know that there was another world outside of my little world. That night, I played "Creep" by Radiohead so many times that I could sing it as if I knew how to speak English even when I did not understand a single word.

It did not take long before Noe and I became best friends. We were so popular in school with our unique hairstyles and the wealth of music knowledge that we had. We were called all types of cool nicknames, which brought us great fame among the students.

Together, we made news every day with our looks and the many activities that we completed. At the freshman five-mile race, we ran together and placed first. To make it look unique, we stopped right before the finish line, only to take one synchronized step and tie the race. At the school homecoming event, we had the best dance moves and danced with many girls. Probably the most memorable event was when we both volunteered to donate fresh semen for our biology class. While at the so-called lab, the teacher had asked if anyone wanted to volunteer to donate semen so that we could look at it under the new microscope that the town had donated to the school. As the heroes we were, we took our small containers and walked to the bathroom, but not before the teacher pulled out an adult magazine from his briefcase. Needless to say, we came back victorious in approximately three minutes.

There was also the one day our biology teacher asked us to bring bunnies for a dissecting exercise. Little did we know that we each had to kill our bunny while in class. The screaming from the girls could be heard all over the school. Our teacher had brought a bottle of ether, a wide plastic container, and a wooden stick. The exercise was simple and disgraceful, pour the ether on a rag, forcefully cover the bunny's face with the rag until it stops fighting, grab the bunny by the legs over the container and proceed to hit it on the head until it dies. The scene was traumatic at best when the first rabbit bled on the plastic container right next to our teacher's desk. I remember feeling sick and sorry for the bunnies and everyone in class. The sound of the stick hitting the back of the bunny's head was heartbreaking. To make matters worse, most students struggled to hit the bunnies hard and only prolonged their death and made them suffer more. I don't know if it was the problems at home that had taught me to numb my feelings or the adrenaline running through my body, but Noe and I volunteered to kill everyone's rabbit out of compassion for them. I figured if I could hit them hard and get it over with sooner with one hit, the bunnies would suffer less than being hit on the head alive multiple times. It was a horrible day, and our reputation increased even more at the expense of those beautiful, furry bunnies. There were stories all over school about how rock music made Noe and

I heartless and savages. Both girls and boys thought of us as cool, intriguing students whom it would be fun to be friends with.

My first high school year could not be any better; even at home things were more stable. My father had left for the United States, once again promising that he would work hard to change our lifestyles. He even promised to send money and to call my grandmother's house every weekend. We knew both promises were false but were very happy to have him leave the house again. Our life without my father was not much different from an economic standpoint, but we had a peaceful life, which meant more than money. It was a forgotten privilege to sleep throughout the night, to not have to sleep with shoes on in case I had to run or with a knife under my pillow for protection and to not worry about the well-being of my mother and siblings.

During that year, I had multiple jobs, one of which I clearly remember: peeling hot peppers. The job itself was boring and monotonous, but the pain in my hands from handling hot peppers was unbearable. I peeled hot peppers for hours, to the point where the pain would not let me sleep very well, even when I wore plastic gloves. The little money I made was used to help my mother, and anything I kept I spent on a couple of cheap rock-band shirts and knockoff rock cassettes. Occasionally, I had enough money left to hang out with Noe and buy delicious street-corner Mexican *elotes,* which is corn with sour cream and chili pepper. We sat and enjoyed the corn at the plaza while we talked about all the girls we wanted to date and the latest rock albums.

One weekend my aunt stopped by the house. She was my father's sister, and she wanted to tell us that my father had called my grandma's house and wanted to talk to us later that day. The plan was to drive us to my grandma's house and wait for six o'clock when my father would call again. Hesitantly and more out of pressure from my aunt, my mother agreed to go. We did not have a phone at our home, so we needed to go to grandma's. But first, we all had to take showers and dress nicely for my grandma, who would always wait for us with overwhelming joy.

"Everyone, let's get ready. We are going to your grandma's house to talk to your father," said my mom.

"Yes, Mom," we responded with an unhappy tone.

My paternal grandmother was an angel. She was a beautiful old lady whose house and clothes always smelled like chamomile tea and wet dirt from her gardens. She had had thirteen children whom she had raised with love and the soul of a passionate mother. Her eyes had already been blurred by the many years she had lived, but they still looked colorful and kind. Her face looked tired from carrying all the problems of the world on her shoulders. Her wrinkled skin always felt soft against my cheeks, which she would kiss as she half-mumbled words explaining how much she missed me. Each of her wrinkles was carefully folded to reveal her age and to conceal her sorrow. Each movement of her body showed her courage and her willingness to hold on to whatever health she had left. She was the daughter of a German mine owner who had returned to Germany after the mining business struggled during the Mexican Revolution. Her luck with men did not improve when she married my grandfather, who abused her and hit her even in their eighties. Her life had been dedicated to her thirteen children, of which my father was the thirteenth. My grandma was a devoted Catholic who placed her faith on many saints and blessed us with every Bible passage she knew every time she saw us. During her last years of life, she suffered from diabetes, which made her lose both of her legs but not her optimistic spirit. Even from that old bed that had lost the smell of chamomile, she jumped out of joy every time she saw us. My aunts never got tired of saying that my siblings and I were her favorite grandchildren. I never knew if they were right, but I always thought that the kindness in her eyes revealed a great amount of pity for us. After all, we were the kids of her reckless son whom she could neither stop loving nor forget about despite all the damage that he had caused to her and us.

That afternoon, she received us with a lovely smile. "Your father wants to talk to you! See, I told you that he loves you greatly. He said that he misses you so much and that he wants to see you." My grandma never got tired of telling us that we needed to forgive my father, as deep inside he was a good man and really loved us. "I think this time he has really changed! Please, Virgin Mary, let it be true. Let it be true, divine mother of God. He even says that he bought a house and that you can come and live with him and learn English! You want to learn English. English is so beautiful!" Six o'clock arrived, and little did I know that this call would change our lives.

"Hello, son," my father said with a kind voice that I have never heard before. "Hi," I responded with a cold and dry tone. After that, he went on for minutes talking about how successful the last months had been for him. I must have said less than ten words during the five minutes we talked. It sounded like he was not taking a single breath while he was talking. There were no pauses nor questions. *Who does he think he is, addressing me like he has been the father of the year?* I thought while I put on a good smile for my grandmother, who looked at me from her bed with watery eyes while she held a rosary with praying hands. Lastly, after my father had spoken to all my siblings, my mother took over the phone. I did not hear her say much during what must have been a thirty-minute-long one-way conversation. After the call ended, she sat by my grandma's bed and began talking slowly with an incredulous look on her face. I did not stay to hear the conversation between the two of them and went on to spend time at my grandmother's gardens.

A couple of days later, my mother talked to my siblings and me about moving to the United States with my father for a few months. "Your father has changed, and he wants us to come and visit him. He even bought a house and has a stable job. He can send bus money for all of us." She went on to say approximately one hundred times, "I don't want you to grow up without a father." As incredulous as I felt hearing my mother say those words, I was not surprised about it. My mother had given my father countless opportunities to come back home and start all over. While many of those opportunities were forced by my father, my mother always believed that my father would change and become a great man.

I would like to think that it was her kindness and her faith in God being able to change him that allowed her to fall into such a vicious cycle. Perhaps it was fear of retaliation, or she simply did not have the courage to stop him every time he came back. My foggy childhood memories remember me feeling very confused every time they kissed and she took him back after he had left for a long time, sometimes even years. Especially when most times he left was after a very violent fight. This time, selfishly, I agreed with her to give him another chance, but only because I wanted to go to the United States. Since I was a child, I had always known about the American dream. Countless times on our street, we heard of someone going to the United States in search of opportunity and progress. It was a place where people could make three dollars per hour, which as a little boy with limited mathematical skills sounded like a lot more than I would make bagging groceries, collecting cardboard, or putting together raffles. Many times, we glanced at the wealth that could be acquired in the United States when people who lived on our street returned with brand-new trucks after spending many months north.

Many people around me had lived the American dream and came back home with enough money to get ahead for a few years. My uncle, for instance, had built a beautiful house with money he saved during one full year of hard work in America. I remember that every weekend, while they made bread, my aunt would cry on my mother's shoulder about my uncle being away from home. "Do you think he will ever return? He may leave us forever," said my aunt, sobbing every time. However, every weekend, she would receive money from my uncle, which she saved joyfully with the goal of building their dream house.

The United States was a country of wealth, technology, fashion, and so many shiny objects that one could have sworn that heaven was not far from it. It was just like the many movies I had watched with the beautiful houses and neighborhoods. There were houses where children had their own room and even a tree house. In that moment when my mother explained herself repeatedly, I had a vision. The United States was the answer to helping my family. I could get a great job and save money to help my mother. I could buy clothes for everyone. I could even buy my mother and me a car. I saw myself driving down the main street of my town with one hand on the steering wheel and the other over the shoulder of a beautiful girl sitting right next to me. I saw myself speaking English fluently, having a conversation with my English teacher, and helping all the beautiful girls in class who struggled with their English homework. I could be another one of those people who reached the dream. I even saw myself marrying a blonde American girl with piercing blue eyes. I could end our economic struggles, and deep inside me, I thought, *I could stop being a burden to my mother who has three other kids to raise.* This last thought was the voice of my self-sufficient self who always felt guilty taking from my mother and felt the pressure of contributing to our humble house. The thoughts came to me rapid-fire while my heart beat faster and faster. It was no different than that moment, when playing chess, where one finds the way to checkmate the opponent. I could see a clear path to win, a clear path to the American dream.

The next few months before school was over felt slow and painful. Every day that I spent in my town was a day when I could have been making money in the United States. I found it useless to go to school and learn anything. My life had been solved with one phone call. Life had shown mercy to me. With such distraction on mind, my grades began to suffer—particularly my biology class, which I was at risk of failing. I had never found myself in this situation, I had always been an honors student. My days at school were spent having fun and not taking anything seriously. I hung out with Noe the whole day and skipped class multiple times to go have fun with friends. In time, I stopped seeing Victor, and the few times I saw him, I found him boring and childish. Once, I ran into him as I hung out with a group friends from school at the plaza, and I felt embarrassed to have him run toward me, hug me, and greet me with a silly and authentic smile. He, as always, looked disheveled and happy. He walked toward me and talked to me like no one was watching and the plaza belonged to him alone, built for him alone. I, on the other hand, looked different, was different. My face had changed; my voice sounded confident and probably even arrogant. However, deep inside I felt like I was a poser in my own clothes. We exchanged a few words for a few minutes. All I recall is his smiley face very close to mine, maybe even too close that it made me feel uncomfortable—too close to the point that I could smell his breath. He was uttering words at a faster rhythm than he would usually talk. I was standing there nodding my head and forcing myself to smile. I was more conscious of my friends who looked with disapproval at my being seen with such strange person. As the minutes went by, I even began to feel hot and began to sweat a bit. I could feel my face getting hot as a drip of sweat went down my temple. My body language must have been so easy to read that even Victor realized what was going on, and with a kind smile, he looked down to the ground, slowed his speech, said good-bye, and left. Why did I let my eagerness to conform with society get in the way of me and my best friend? There is a list of actions that I have done in my life when I felt deeply ashamed of myself. This day was added to my memory as one that needed to be challenged by my values and morals. I only spoke to Victor one more time before I left to the United States and was not capable of apologizing.

As the end of the year came closer and closer, I only got more excited about our trip to the United States. However, when my grades before finals came out, I realized that I was in trouble and at risk of failing many classes, especially my biology class. My mother was screaming as if passing this class was a matter of life or death. "You will go to your room and study for your final test, day and night, until you learn all the content! You are not to come out of there until you are confident that you will pass with an A. If you fail this class, I swear we will not go to the United States. I don't care what else is going on around you, you will always prioritize school. Imagine what people would say if they learn that my son—a teacher's son—is failing school! Not in my house!" Angry, I studied for days and forced myself to learn everything that I had been neglecting to pay attention to. I knew my mother was serious when she said that we would not go visit my father if I failed my class, so I could not afford to fail the class. On the day of the test, I said a prayer before taking the test and took plenty of time to answer each question. My life and my future depended on a test again. A week after, the results were in, and I had barely passed the class by acing the final test. On the day my mother received the results, sitting on the couch at home, she made me promise her that over all things I would never neglect school. I looked my mother in the eyes, tired from the stress of the days that I had waited for my grades, and said, "I promise, Mom."

PART 2

CHAPTER 1

Newcomers

UNLIKE MANY IMMIGRANT stories, mine does not start with a coyote smuggling me through a dark hot desert during a three-day walk or traveling in the trunk of a car. There are no side deals on the corner of a Mexican barrio or neighborhood with any immigrant smugglers, jumping any fences or swimming any rivers. I did not ride on the roof of a train, crawl through a dark tunnel, or go through the Mexican–American border hidden in an eighteen-wheeler cargo trailer with other fifty people. Instead, I came to the United States legally. Yes, the twenty-two-hour trip by bus was incredibly uncomfortable. Those seats did not recline more than two inches, and sitting next to the smelly bathroom was not ideal. However, millions of immigrants can only dream about the circumstances under which I came to the United States.

Unlike many immigrant stories, when I first arrived, I did not have to struggle to find a place to live. I did not live with twenty other people in a one-bedroom, one-bath apartment. I did not beg for food or shelter or receive any help from the government to get going. When I arrived in the United States, there was a bedroom and a clean bed waiting for me. Ironically, my father, the man who had wasted most of his life on alcohol and drugs, was waiting for us with a clean house. The beginning of my American journey was not anything that can be made into a movie. Perhaps that should have been a clear sign that something was wrong. Life was simply too good to be true, and while God had a plan to shower me with blessings, getting me ready for such gifts required turbulences, tests, mistakes, scarcity, pain, and many other innate life ingredients.

It was the early 2000s during a warm summer when we arrived. The California valley received us with its display of many climate types and scenery within a day's drive. I remember we went from a rocky desert to a flat one, which ended at the hills of an uncountable number of mountains. The mountains were pale at first but transitioned into all types of blue colors with patches of snow at the top. The valley itself was flat for the most part, but quickly the abundance of rocks, desert sand, and mountains turned into an abundant number of palm trees, roads, stores, and an endless number of houses that disappeared into the horizon without reaching its end.

There were cars, many cars, and they all looked like they had just been washed, without any dust on them. There were many newer cars; there were many gorgeous-looking houses like the ones I had seen in movies when I was younger.

There were people of all colors and shapes and sizes and wearing different styles of fashion. I saw many people through the window of that dirty and uncomfortable bus and most looked like they were on a mission, eager to arrive somewhere. Most of them with their windows rolled up, which made me assume the weather was not very hot. I thought, "How can they not be hot with their windows rolled up like that?" The magnificence and luxury of car air conditioning was not part of my knowledge at that time. It was simply something that I had not thought about. Before I knew it, there were fewer palm trees and more concrete and asphalt. Yes, all roads were paved and smooth. I thought, *This is what flying must feel like, smooth and soothing.* The noise created by the spin of the tires in contact with the freeway was no less than a well-tuned musical instrument played by the bus driver. That concrete jungle outside my window was a work of art intentionally built to impress me and receive me on that day. The roads were traced by masters of their trade, and each house showed a respect for universal architectural rules. These were the commonsense rules that never challenge the laws of physics and the consequences when violated. There was no trash on the street or anywhere to be seen. It was a miraculous act of discipline and structure in front of my incredulous eyes, where every item—every house, light, post, yard, building—was designed and built by a committed hand, an expert hand, a blessed hand.

As we entered the busy cities, I saw among the buildings empty patches of land full of people running, playing, laughing, and more. What was more impactful to me was that there was green grass on them—they were parks. I saw the richness of the soil and how unbelievably fruitful it was. I saw houses with water shooting from the ground like in the movies and watering their green and spacious yards that had a separate paved place to park their cars. I saw walkways on each street and kids and women riding their shiny bikes with ease. I quickly noticed the respect for street signs and the fact that each street had a new-looking sign. I thought, *Street children who beg for money or food or clean windshields must not have a problem walking among the idling cars waiting for a green light. It must be much easier to beg for money here.* At the time I did not stop to notice that such travesty in our current society did not exist here anymore. I also noticed the absence of graffiti on most walls and buildings. I did not see any wandering dogs or cats, at which point I stopped my spinning mind abruptly to question the lack of rebar on every single house and business window. *There must be a lot of crime here!* I thought. *How do people keep criminals from breaking into their houses?* While such scenery could not be like the golden streets of heaven described in the Bible, entering the United States was the closest to it that I had ever been exposed to.

My wondering and unbelieving eyes did not stop marveling at such a place when we finally arrived. The final stop was at a shopping center where the bus company had a small office among the many other businesses. There were Chinese, Vietnamese, and Mexican restaurants right next to each other and many clothing stores with clear empty glass windows. As we left the bus, I continued to notice the wealth of such an amazing country in anyone and everything that crossed my way. I saw clean, new shoes being worn literally by everyone, which I quickly attributed to the fact that, based on the overwhelming number of cars, everyone most likely had a car and therefore walked less. Everyone also looked clean and well-dressed in properly fitted clothing. I did not see a single person with white spots on their cheeks or stained teeth. The floors in the stores were clean, there were public bathrooms everywhere, and restaurant employees were in uniforms and even wearing gloves. One could not tell if a car was on or off as there was not any smoke coming out the back, shaking, or loud cranking noises.

My father picked us up on what in Mexico would have been an almost-new car, but here it was an old model. The car looked clean and recently vacuumed but smelled like way too many little pine tree deodorants. We all had to wear seat belts, and my father was sober, without a drink between his legs. He looked healthy and happy. His widows peak was more defined, but his face looked younger, and his teeth very white as he gave us a joyful smile. We took off with a quick turn into the busy avenue that made the rosary hanging from his rear-view mirror swing aggressively left to right. I don't remember much of that car drive, as my brain was starting to overload with such scenery and questions. All I remember is that my father did not allow a single second of silence as he talked and swung his hands in all types of motions. His hand movements looked decisive and confident while his lips seemed to press too hard on each other in between words as his tongue struggled and worked hard to keep them moist.

It could have been thirty minutes or an hour before we arrived home. It was a small melon-colored two-bedroom, one-bath single-family home with a small porch and red Spanish tiles for a roof. My siblings and I would share one of the bedrooms while my father and mother would take the other. There was very little furniture in the house, but we sat on an old couch in the living room where my father talked about his two jobs and how great life would be in the United States, to which my mother quickly reminded him that we would not stay here forever. "This is only a temporary vacation," she said. My father stopped, stared at my mother for a few seconds, and agreed to her comment with a cautious smile. "Let me show you around," my father said. "Yay!" screamed my two little brothers, jumping off the couch, while my sister and I stood up and walked with our hands behind our backs, still hesitant to believe what we were seeing. After my father showed us around the house and green yard, we sat for another couple of hours to talk about the life we were about to begin together while my siblings ran and wrestled with each other on the carpet. The house was way bigger than our house in Mexico, which provided a great chasing and wrestling environment. The carpet itself was a thing of the movies, and my toes could not stop rubbing it just like my siblings could not stop rolling on it.

While I listened to everything my father and mother said, I was truly in shock to see so much in so little time. Through the noise of the conversation, more than once in my head I questioned my father's soberness and our short-term memories about all the abuse we had sustained from him. I was simply unhappy with this feeling of peace, gratitude, and hope. It could not be this good, life was always ready to betray us, and I should not allow myself to give into my father's promises. Could it be that my mother was right all these years about my father changing for good? Did I not see what my mother saw? Were my feelings toward my father wrong? Was I a bad person for having a hard time forgiving? Why should I forgive him? After all, I am his responsibility since I am his son! I did not choose to be born! Why am I not able to feel anything for him? Why am I feeling hope? Why do I feel like I don't have any resentment when I should? Is this wrong? For the first hours upon our arrival, there was extreme chaos in my mind and a mix of many contradicting feelings that, in the end, left me numb once again. Perhaps, at the time, numbness was my way of coping with life and my best survival tool—one that had carried me on for as long as I had a conscience.

Long into the conversation, my father made eye contact with me and explained that I would have to attend school while I was there and that I would have to work to help support the family. All ideas were well received by my overloaded mind except the moment when he said I would have to grow a mustache and stop shaving, which I immediately disagreed with. My puberty mustache left unshaved looked like a raccoon's whiskers, so I was not happy with the advice. It would be impossible to get a girlfriend at school. My father explained that it was illegal for me to work eight hours a day at that age and that I would have to do it "under the table" until I was eighteen. Growing a mustache would make me look older and would mitigate any concerns about me being underage. My negative reaction to the mustache immediately triggered my father, who began screaming at me, except he was not drunk and his words were uncharacteristically true words of advice. Of course, at that time, he sounded like a monster with no regard for my personal happiness, and his loud voice immediately brought back a feeling of fear and anger within me.

"You have no idea how lucky you are to come to this country and have a house and a family to support you. You don't know anything about how things work here, so you have to listen to me. We come to this country to work hard at all costs and under all types of sacrifices. Be thankful for being here, and listen to my advice. Your days will be packed with responsibilities. You will go from school to work and come home to sleep only to wake up and do the same thing the next day. If you want to be here, this is the sacrifice that you will have to make. You will study and you will learn English. You are no longer a child! If you want a better job than the one you are about to have and to truly succeed, you will need to learn a new language and adapt to this country. We are not from here, but you will adapt and contribute," he said.

"But we are not staying here forever," I responded with a defeated voice, and I stopped short of saying anything else.

My siblings and mother had that old look of fear on their faces after my father had raised his voice, so I decided to deescalate the situation by staying quiet. That was the moment when I realized that I was not on a vacation and that my father, while he did not seem like a drunk anymore, was still volatile and, more importantly, in control.

My first job in the United States began the day after I arrived. My father took me to a pizza place where he was the cook during his afternoon job. I was quickly hired as the bus boy, with the responsibility to clean and wash more plates than I had ever seen in my whole life. The pace was fast and furious, which made the hours pass fast without much time to think but only to keep up with the load. There were dishwashing machines that I never thought could exist and a kitchen that matched no other ever built, full of stainless steel and advanced tools that made me feel like I was living in the future or in some form of spaceship. *If only my mother would have had anything close to this technology, her life would have been much easier and her hands much softer,* I thought while remembering my mother's hands bleeding under each finger nail from washing too many clothes and dishes by hand every day of the week. I must have seen thousands of families stop by with ferocious appetites. However, it always felt as if they were rushing, and what was worse, they did not seem to notice how much of a blessing walking into such a clean and well-built restaurant was. They all acted as if it was expected to be that way, as if it was within their entitlement to be in such place and enjoy such great service and food. However, the joy of eating delicious pizzas did not show much in their eyes. Being there was not new, affording their meals was not worth celebrating, the condition of the restaurant was not worth admiring, and it was as if they had grown emotionless to the blessings that they had. There was a lack of perspective and gratitude for the life that they had been given, replaced by an air of entitlement that made them look hungry, but never truly like they were enjoying their meals. They would swallow but never truly chew and stop to taste each flavor. They would leave without complaint about the food or service but not joyful for the day. They would laugh to make more noise and to empathize with their friends and family, but never because their soul reminded them of how blessed they were to be there. It did not take me long to realize that in this new world, many people only pretended to be happy and that each new activity only gave them a temporary state of satisfaction before moving on with their next goal. Their hunger could not be satisfied with food because they had never been hungry. Their wants could only fulfill them temporarily because they were all vain. Their humbleness had been conquered and replaced with entitlement, as if it was their right to have, to laugh, to own, to be full, and to be blessed.

* * *

Children, like my mother always told me, this world does not owe you anything. You must earn and fight for your accomplishments. Entitlement and lack of gratitude will not allow you to truly enjoy life the way God wants you to. You cannot celebrate your accomplishments if you did not work hard to earn them. You cannot truly value something that did not require sacrifice and effort. Through your mother and me, may God give us health to raise you and be with you to support you and celebrate both your wins and failures. However, never forget that every breath you take is a blessing that comes from God; be thankful. God says that a single leaf from a tree will not move but per His will. You were blessed before you were born, and such an overwhelming number of blessings may leave you emotionless and numb to how much we have and how lucky we are. Be thankful for His word, for each meal, for your family, for every awakening, for every journey, for every failure, for every success, for every breath. Recognize that He has given us so much. Never allow yourself to feel deserving of more, but rather deserving of less, for even in scarcity, He always has a purpose full of love and mercy.

* * *

It was on my second month or so that I learned about the price of each pizza, which I quickly translated to Mexican pesos, followed by a shocking realization. It would take me one full week of work in Mexico to afford a one-topping pizza. When I was paid for the first time, I realized that I had just earned one month's worth of work in Mexico in one week. Needless to say, the math did not make any sense, but all the stories I had heard as a boy about the American dollars were true. People in this country were wealthy and unbelievably blessed. God had blessed this nation in ways that I struggle to articulate or understand even to this day as I write this book for you.

While I was the one working, my father cashed my checks, took most of my money for the house and left me with a few dollars weekly that I happily used for clothes, snacks, and to test every single burger from all fast-food places that I could walk to on my one day off, Tuesday.

During my first day off from work, my mother, my siblings, and I walked to the nearest high school to begin my enrollment process. My eyes could not believe what I was seeing! The school itself was the size of one whole city. There were buildings of all sizes built with a Colonial architectural style. There were long areas of green grass and tall healthy trees all over the place. The school looked quiet and empty, and the gentle wind of the day made the trees dance, with their leaves pointing aggressively toward one side right before relaxing and surrendering to the pull of gravity. There was not any trash or graffiti; the shape of each building was well planned and in harmony with anything that my eyes could see. As we walked into the administration building, there were long hallways with shiny floors that revealed our profile so clearly, almost like a mirror. Every corner of that school had been polished and fully equipped to protect students against the elements. The smell of new books, pencils, brick, paper, and wood was so delightful that it had the potential to be bottled and sold as a unisex cologne for the intellectual.

Surprisingly, everyone spoke Spanish and looked Hispanic. After filling out multiple forms and taking a couple of tests, I was assigned to the newcomers program—a program designed for immigrants who had just arrived in the country and whose English was not good enough to make it to the standard high school classes. The Newcomers school, while located at the same place, was a building on the back side of the school, facing the high school cafeteria. It was a building that in Mexico could have passed for a town hall or some form of museum.

I spent my first months at the Newcomers school learning English and taking standard high school classes with a little bit of translation help. Our teachers were so smart, kind, and patient that my heart melts as I remember that great season of my life. At Newcomers, I met people from all over the world and built friendships that last until this day, even when our first way of communication, not having a language in common, was all hand motions and noises.

Each student at Newcomers had a humble story to tell, usually full of terror and gratitude for the opportunity to be there. While there were some rebels in the group, of the one hundred plus students, almost everyone understood the opportunity that we had been given.

While my plan was not to stay, there were many of them who would never have a chance to travel to their countries again. There was Karim, who was there thanks to political asylum as his whole family, but parents and siblings, were killed by terrorists somewhere in the Middle East. There was Sarah, a cute Chinese girl whose parents had moved to the United States in order to be able to have more than one kid. There was Tamara, who came from Colombia, fleeing the cartel violence in Medellín. Denys had escaped from the hands of the MS-13, a merciless gang back in El Salvador that recruits young children and kills those who refuse to join. There was Victoria, who came from Argentina after her parents lost everything to a corrupt government. During lunch, we sat together like brothers and sisters; with broken English, noises, and hand motions, collaboratively we helped each other tell stories. Jim (who was from Vietnam and whose real name was something that I cannot spell or pronounce) would help Sarah translate some words, which Tamara could write down. Victoria could then pronounce these and, in return, translate back to me, and on and on. We were a great team.

It was during those lunches that I learned the first of many mind-boggling immigrant stories. There was Paco, who came across the border by crawling in a tunnel for two full days, in the dark, grabbing to the ankle of the person right in front of him, who in turn grabbed onto the person in front of him, all together making a group of more than twenty people. Paco did not see light for two days in that dark tunnel with limited oxygen while he rubbed his knees on urine and feces from the people in front of him. He grabbed onto that ankle and pushed through the dark until he came out free and ready to begin a new life on the other side. There was Alberto, who traveled through the Arizona desert in the trailer container of an eighteen-wheeler for one full day. He explained that there were so many people in there that no one could sit down for the lack of space. He slowed down his breathing, preserving the little oxygen they had, and peed in his pants twice when he could not hold it anymore. He was so dehydrated when he arrived that he was taken to the hospital. There was Juan, who after walking in the desert with a coyote for three days and two nights, was placed in a transition house that the Mexican cartel controlled. At this house, his short body frame became an advantage when he was able to fit under the one and only piece of furniture in the four-bedroom house, a small bed. Getting under the bed was the best break he could have had as he was able to extend his body fully to sleep. Everywhere else in the house, with so many people waiting to be picked up by their relatives, there was literally no space to lay down unless you rested your body on someone else's legs. Dirty, hungry, thirsty, scared, and emotionally devastated during such a harsh journey, Juan covered his ears and protected his head from getting hit with the bouncing mattress as the cartel lords raped as many women and children as they pleased in front of everyone in the room. The perpetrators were armed and rested, and there was not anything that any of the tired, restless, weak, and hungry people in the room could do about it but cry.

Day after day, I learned more about my friends and built deeper friendships. Day after day, I worked hard at learning the language and doing my best at work. Working until ten or eleven at night every day and going to school at the same time left me without any energy to do anything else. On my days off, I would rent VHS movies and watch them with subtitles on so that I could repeat and learn every word. I was on a mission to learn English, and no one could stop me. Many times, I stared at the high school side of the school and promised myself that I would get transferred soon. While I loved being at Newcomers, I knew that the real challenge would begin when all the language support was taken away. I was also extremely attracted to the many blue-eyed girls that attended high school, and I could not wait to be able to talk to one. I can say that blue eyed girls were my platonic love.

After less than six months at Newcomers, I was made aware of my transfer to high school. I was also asked to speak at the Newcomers graduation. On that night, my mother and siblings sat in the front row with watery eyes and loud claps. Once again, I found myself in front of a podium facing a large audience. The speech I had prepared was a page and a half long and written in English. While my mother rocked her body back and forth, rubbing her hands on her thighs and murmuring a prayer, I felt proud to deliver my first English speech and thanked God for this first milestone. Now it was time to move on.

CHAPTER 2

The Chase

IT WAS ON a Saturday night after a long day of work that my mother handed me a letter from Victor. My eyes could not believe that he had written to me, and neither did my hands, which held the envelope hesitantly for longer than my brain had ordered them to open it. His handwriting had not changed, I realized that it was the real Victor who had sent that letter the moment I opened it. Shaky circular *A*s and *E*s, and uneven paragraphs full of words that were only noises and one could not find in a dictionary. Victor had the ability to communicate noises and facial expressions through his writing—and more importantly, emotions. How can the boy whom I named my best friend and later ignored because of social pressure still remember me and take the time to write me a letter and address me as his best friend? My guilt had only increased from the last time that I saw him. In his letter, he explained that life was great and that his plan was to move to Mexico City to pursue a career in acting. He went on to talk about how much he missed me, and he provided details of classes he was taking and more. He even included a section in English to test how well I was doing learning a new language. Once the initial emotion of finding my mother with a letter from Victor was gone, my exhaustion came back, and I went straight to bed. Perhaps it was the pace of my life at the time, perhaps it was my guilt about the way I ignored him while I was still in Mexico, but I never responded to Victor's letter. I was a bad friend.

Nearly six months had gone by, and our American journey was steady. While we ate well and had a stable handful of months with my father, the economics of our house were not glamorous. We lived paycheck to paycheck and barely made it every month. My father had two jobs, but he made a few pennies more than minimum wage, so the money was always tight. My mother would accumulate as many coupons as possible throughout the week and buy most of our groceries from dollar stores. We did not have any luxuries at home, and what was worse, we did not have any savings. However, such a limited lifestyle was a better alternative than Mexico and certainly an upgrade.

Sometime during the first months we were there, my father began to show signs of a changing behavior. It started with his days off, when he would drink from morning to night, spending money that we very much needed. He also lied to my mother, who helped administer the money and pay bills, about how much money he made. Eventually, he drank and became slightly aggressive but still went to bed without much drama. As the months went by, the beginning of a new period took place on a Friday night, when he did not return home after we had been paid for our week's work. The next day, he showed up early, looking drunk and tired. When my mother dared to ask him for money to pay the bills that were due that weekend, he screamed belligerently and pushed her out of the room violently, shutting the door loudly. There was a quick moment of silence before my mother broke down in tears. It was more than silence—it was a reality check. It was the day when our fears came to life and resurrected all the emotions and memories of a not-too-distant past. It was time to leave. The moment we prayed would never arrive was now here, and it was as real as the flashbacks that relentlessly reminded me of who he was and who he would always be. I was right—it was all hopes and dreams, and we were naive to believe that he had changed. My father had removed his deceitful mask.

Moneyless and resourceless, we would have to wait until we had enough money to leave. The reality was that my father was in control, and we did not even have the resources to go back home. My mother and I dusted it off and went on with our week, pretending to ignore what had happened; but thoughtfully and in secret, without telling my siblings, we planned our escape back to Mexico. We needed to leave, and we needed to leave soon. The plan was to take all the money from the following week of work, assuming he would not go and spend it all again, and buy bus tickets to go back home. We would wait for him to go to work and then leave in secret, but not before writing a letter that we would leave on the table of an empty house. The letter would explain that we did not tolerate such behavior anymore and that we would rather leave before his violent actions hurt any of us, including himself. We no longer had the patience that we once had to put up with it and forgive him repeatedly.

Like most true-life events and movies, nothing ever goes according to plan. During the week leading up to the great escape to Mexico, my father continued to act irrationally and drank most days of the week. Surprisingly, he had money for beer but not to pay the rent. The change was so drastic that in one week, he lost one of his jobs, his morning job, as he was caught refilling his soda cup with draft beer right before getting in the car and driving back home. On my day off, my friends and I stopped by the house only to find him smoking crack in the shed out back. I was so embarrassed by such a discovery that I cried in front of my friends, followed by a fake laugh, pretending everything was okay. That same day, my mother and siblings had to move out of the house and sleep at a friend's house from church. I stayed home with the excuse that I had to go to school and work the next day, and I was old enough to take care of myself. My mother screamed at the sky when I refused to go with her. However, from the time I was a little boy, life had prepared me to live life as an adult, replacing many childhood moments with tests and hardships that would eventually allow me to mature sooner than a child or a teenager should. We are taught that there is an order of seasons in life, but in the end, God guides our way through paths that almost never align with our expectations. My life was not an exception.

I waited until late to come back home, only to find my father with another woman in the house. She was a skinny old blonde lady who looked like she had not slept in weeks. Her bony face was covered with all types of red and previously erupted pimples, and her mouth moved in circles, as if she was trying to get something off her nose or cheeks or perhaps even chewing on something sticky. Her clothes were sparkling and two sizes too small revealing her malnourished legs and shoulders. She made eye contact yet did not see you. She walked straight, but her steps looked wobbly. Her body was there, but her soul had left her a long time ago. I ran out of the house and stayed with my neighbor Ricardo, who snuck me in through the window and allowed me to sleep on the floor of his room.

During the next days before payday, my mother returned home to pick up some clothes while my father was working and to get everything ready for the departure, doing her best to not allow my father to notice. On Friday, I attended school just like any other normal day and went to work right after. I washed dishes faster than any day before and was done cleaning tables a few minutes before my shift was over. While my father cleaned his cooking space, I walked into our manager's office to collect our money, which he always handed to my father. My heart was pumping fast and hard while I uttered with a soft and quiet voice, "Mike, can I please have our money, we need to leave as soon as my dad is done cleaning, so he asked me to get it from you." I was praying that my father would not hear me ask. His workstation was only a few steps away from Mike's office. Mike, a big, tall guy whose shirt was always dirty in the belly section with chicken wing grease and pizza dough, stood up from his chair slower than he ever had before, stretched both arms, fixed his apron, and reached the top shelf to grab an envelope full of bills. As he sat down again and counted the money, I was sure that he could hear my heart beating against my chest or see its pulse in my hands and neck. Everything slowed down in that moment except my heart and my father, whom I could hear rapidly putting the cleaning tools away. Finally, after calculating hours and multiplying numbers on his loud calculator, he handed me the money. "Good job," he said with a crooked smile, one hand on the bills and the other one fixing the pressure of his apron on his belly.

I took that money and ran outside, to a set of stairs a few yards away from the main entrance of the pizzeria. That afternoon I had gone to work on my Rollerblades, which was my one and only way of getting from school to work. Every day I would Rollerblade about four miles uphill to get to work on the smooth walkways of the city, on one of the longest and straightest avenues at the foothill of the mountain. Just as I finished putting my Rollerblades on as fast as I could with my shaky hands and barely catching my breath, my father pushed the door open abruptly and in panic. "WHERE DO YOU THINK YOU ARE GOING WITH MY MONEY!" he screamed as he rushed toward the set of stairs where I had sat to change. Before he could get any closer to me, I jumped off the stairs, struggling to put my backpack on, and began Rollerblading backward at a great speed. In a matter of seconds, I was in the middle of a chase where an angry alcoholic father ran as fast as he could to get his beer and drug money but was just too slow to catch me. I had always been a great Rollerblader, but months of turning such a hobby into my only way of transportation had made me only better.

Regardless of how fast I was, running away from a car took much more than skills. When my father saw that he could not catch me, he went straight for the car and began to chase me on the streets. The same avenue that took me to work uphill every day repaid me for all my efforts and sweat in that single moment. Even my father's reckless driving that violated every street sign was no match for the gravity pull that pushed me away for him. That night, I was unstoppable.

I lost my father after a fearless persecution worth making into a commercial or movie scene. However, the chase was worthless when I still needed to go home. Something inside me—something not very smart or thoughtful—told me that I could go home and explain to my father that I simply wanted to make sure that the money went toward the mortgage and that under no circumstances did I intend to keep it. After much consideration, I decided to go home and have my friend Carlos who lived up the street come with me for moral support. *Maybe*, I thought, *if he sees me with my friend, he will hold back on his anger.*

I had met Carlos during my first week at Newcomers. Carlos, his mother, and his siblings had come from Mexico after his father almost killed his mother one Halloween night when he returned home drunk. That was not the first time his father had hit his mother, but it was certainly the last. The next morning, after his mother was released from the hospital, his whole family pitched in to pay a coyote who could take them to the United States, where they could hide from his father forever. Carlos and I bonded immediately when we learned about our alcoholic fathers and the many struggles that we faced growing up. He was a hyperactive teenager who could not get good grades at school and dreamed of having his first car. Carlos was a good friend and not a stranger to the types of circumstances under which I found myself that day.

To our surprise, my father was not home when we arrived, which made it easier for us to get in, and it allowed me to change my clothes and get some stuff ready for my upcoming departure. Later that night, while my friend was still with me, we saw the lights of my father's car pull into the driveway. The time had come to face him.

Let's just say that there was not much to talk about. My father went straight to my room where Carlos and I waited with a shut door. My friend lay on my bed comfortably, while I sat on the carpet with my back against the bed, shaky and anxious. As I heard him approach the door, his steps were so fast that I barely had a second to stand before he opened the door with the necessary force to smash through it. The same force that he used to turn that knob could have been used to put his hand through it, and frankly, the sound that door made was not much different than that of a strong boot kicking it down. He looked sweaty and unkempt, and his hair was tousled, which made his forehead look bigger than normal and his widow's peak much wider. His eyes were fixated on mine with deep uncontrollable anger. He came so close to my face that I could feel and smell his warm, intoxicated breath on my face. His pupils were constricted, surrounded by his bloodshot eyes, and revealing an evil look. In a split second, my heart raced and began to tighten my throat, which in turn forced me to take fast shallow breaths. Out of nowhere, my friend got in the middle of both of us by forcefully squeezing in between us while facing my father. I could not allow my friend to get hurt, so I quickly pulled him behind me. At this point my father turned his sight toward Carlos, and with a violent, unexpected move, he raised his fist and punched him in the face. The punch was so forceful that both my friend and I were struck by it. Carlos got the worst of it and went flying back to my bed, where he originally lay.

The last time that I felt that overwhelming amount of anger that I felt in that moment was the day when my father had hit my mother in front of me. The force of his hit was so strong that my mother hit the back of her head on the floor. That was the day I lost control over my body and chased him down the street as he took off in our car. Here I was, years after, resurrecting the same level of anger under a situation that, while it did not match what he did to my mother, made feelings that I had not forgotten about become more real. Such emotions going through my head and body transported me back to that day when I could not catch him to give him what he deserved. On this day, there was a big difference: he was right in front of me, and I was no longer a boy. I was not an adult either, nor did I possess the strength that my father did. However, I was not a normal fifteen-year-old. My body had been forced to mature through the many efforts that I had demanded of it, working since the time I was eight. I was also sober, and while I was blinded by anger, my goal was very clear: to hurt him.

It could have been even before Carlos landed on the bed and my father brought his arm back from above my shoulder that the speed of my tight, angry fists began to impact his face and body violently with toxic hate and strength. My mouth made noises that only a trapped angry animal could make while my tears rolled down my cheeks and splashed everywhere with my vicious movements. I did not stop until I pushed him and punched him out of the house to the patio, at which point, he collapsed on the concrete ground, only to stand up quickly, struggling to regain his stability. I then realized that I was in danger as my strength was not enough to defeat him. My feelings quickly turned into fear and a glimpse of guilt for hurting my father. It was then when I screamed with all the power of my lungs, "I HATE YOU! I HAVE ALWAYS HATED YOU, YOU SELFISH PIECE OF SHIT! YOU HAVE MADE OUR LIVES SO MISERABLE! YOU ARE NOT HALF THE MAN YOU CLAIM TO BE, AND NO MATTER HOW MUCH TIME GOES BY, I WILL ALWAYS HATE YOU!" When I finished, I noticed his eyes changed from anger to sadness with his shoulders slowly slouching. Seeing that he had lowered his guard and that my words had hurt him more than my punches, I slowly approached him until my chest touched his, and looking directly at his eyes, I screamed again right in his face, "I HATE YOU!"

Carlos grabbed me by the shoulder to signal me that it was time to run, and so we did. Before I turned to the sidewalk as I was leaving the house, I looked back once more, only to find my father in the same place, looking down at the ground with a defeated posture. Who would have known that this would be the last time that my father and I would see each other again?

I never told my mother what had happened on that night. I also convinced my friend not to call the cops on my father, who would face jail time if they found out that he hit a couple of fifteen-year-old teenagers while intoxicated and on who knows what other drugs.

With barely enough money for bus tickets and meals to get back to Mexico, I had the most life-changing idea: I should stay in the United States so that I could help my mother and siblings from here. As you can imagine, the idea was not well received by my mother, who responded also with the most solid no that I had ever heard from her. However, that was an answer that I was expecting, and I knew how to respond and convince my mother.

My father had a sister who had moved to the United States many years ago and stayed in touch with us over the years, my aunt Liliana. When we temporarily moved to the United States, my aunt would frequently visit us and even help my father when facing financial issues. She was the most successful woman in my father's family and the only one to go to university out of thirteen siblings. She was married to a great man, my uncle Luis. My uncle was a war veteran with a very mellow personality and an impeccable work ethic. Both had worked hard to build their wealth and were the perfect example of a successful American family. They lived in a beautiful house not too far from us but in a very affluent area. Their kids were positioned to live a steady life with successful careers and great parents.

My aunt knew about my father's addictions and violent behavior toward us and always stayed in touch to make sure that we were well. She also never wasted an opportunity to scream at my father, "YOU ARE A GROWN-UP MAN NOW! YOU MUST CHANGE FOR YOUR FAMILY. LOOK AT THOSE BEAUTIFUL KIDS YOU HAVE. FIGHT FOR THEM!" More than once, my aunt told us how much she hated helping my father, but she could never stop because of a promise that she had made to my grandmother in the minutes before she died.

"Promise me that you will help my son and his family when I am not here, Liliana," whispered my grandmother with the last breath she had while squeezing her old wooden rosary between my aunt's hands.

"I promise, Mother," answered my aunt, taking on the responsibility to continue to enable my father's addictions.

My aunt owned real estate throughout the city and always had some of it rented for additional income. My plan was simple, I would call my aunt and ask her to rent me a room at one of her properties. I could then stay to finish my school and save some money to help my mother. My aunt, remembering the promise that she had made to my grandmother, accepted to rent me a room and helped me stay.

My mother cried so much that her eyes were swollen and bloodshot as she waved at me through the window of the same dirty bus that had taken us to America. My siblings had a quiet and solemn look as they waved goodbye to me as well. To this day, I am not sure how I convinced my mother to leave me here. Was it that I acted and looked much older that I was? Was it that she knew that I could have a better future? Maybe it was as simple as knowing that I would stay near a family member who cared about me. As the bus took off, I held my tears for as long as I could so that my mother would not see me sad. When the bus was finally out of sight, I sat on the street curb, weak and shaky. I rested my elbows on my thighs, bent my head down, and cried uncontrollably, with accelerated breaths that trembled my whole body. Here I was again, at the beginning of another season in my life.

CHAPTER 3

Guilty by Accusation

IT WAS STILL a little dark outside when my alarm sounded. It was an old radio alarm with bright-red blinking numbers that made a detestable sound. Tired and groggy, I rolled on my bed and slammed the alarm a few times without opening my eyes until it went off. I was at a room of an empty house that my aunt and her husband had just finished fixing. Their plan was to put it up for sale in the next few months, at which point I would have to move to a different house. My aunt always had a few houses available to rent. My bed was a stained, bare twin mattress with an old translucent sheet laid on the new carpet floor in the middle of the room. My aunt disliked it when I put the mattress near any of the walls as they could get stained or scratched from it. All my clothes were folded on the carpet floor in one corner of the room, right next to a small carboard box where I had transported them there. There were no pictures on the walls or any other furniture in the room. The rest of the house looked just as empty, including bathrooms, living room, and especially the kitchen, where I was not allowed to cook. Cooking could stain the floors, the stove, or the cabinets, which were all brand-new. There were plastic mats laid all over the carpet floor, tracing and protecting any heavy foot traffic area. My aunt wanted to make sure that the carpet would not get stained or dirty while I was there.

I was also not alone. There was a middle-aged lady who lived in a different room under the same circumstances: an empty room with a mattress lying on the floor and any belongings laid on the floor, away from the walls. She had a son who would come and visit her sometimes. He was one loud kid without manners whom she had to keep outside so that he would not destroy or dirty the house. She always looked tired and lonely. I always thought that something was wrong with her based on her twitchy behavior and the way she insatiably licked her lips all day. My thoughts about her were confirmed the day that she asked if I knew someone who could get her some cocaine. Why did she ask me? It could have been that she was desperate to find it and she did not care who she asked for it. Life was too busy for me to put any thought into it, so I said no, ignored her, and moved on with my life.

Tired and struggling to wake up, I forced myself to shower and get ready for school. It was my sixteenth birthday, but not even the memorable date helped me feel any less tired. It was also my second month alone in the country. In that time, I had switched jobs to a local grocery store, where I collected and pushed shopping carts back into the store until 11:00 p.m. every day of the week except Mondays.

School was not going so well, especially my first-period class (to which I was usually late) and my last-period class (which I sometimes would leave early from so that I could make it to work on time). I did homework late at night or during my break times or any other time I could squeeze it in. I had quit my job at the pizzeria after the owner had screamed at me on a Sunday afternoon in front of all the clients and employees as I pushed my little busboy cart back into the kitchen. We were so busy on that day that each trip to the main floor demanded that I fill my cart with as many plates and cups as possible. During one of my trips back to the kitchen, my cart was so full that a few plates fell off the top as I was trying to avoid a couple of kids running to the playground. The owner, an overweight, middle-aged angry lady with short spiky hair and a loud, mean voice screamed at me, "WHAT ARE YOU DOING, IDIOT? YOU ARE GOING TO HURT SOMEONE WITH THAT FULL CART! GET BACK IN THE KITCHEN AND WASH THE PLATES!"

Over the years, with the many jobs I had had, I knew that there were bad bosses everywhere. There was the lady at the nuts store that caught me eating a sugar-coated pecan and took half a day off my paycheck. There was the foreman at the chili processing plant who would always underpay us and pocket some of our money. There was the lady who owned the cake store who would make me count all the doughnuts at the end of the day and would charge any missing ones off my check. There were these and many other examples, but none of them had ever embarrassed me in front of so many people, especially all those pretty blonde girls eating pizza with their parents on that busy Sunday. I walked my cart right into the kitchen, took my apron off, thanked everyone for the opportunity to work there, and quit.

If there is one clear thing that I remember about that season of my life, it is being very tired and hungry. Weekend mornings or on Mondays, during my day off from work, I would walk to the laundromat with my carboard box and wash my work shirts and any other dirty clothes. I would also hang out with friends and pretended to be a normal teenager, not this sixteen-year-old working a full-time job, living in an empty, sad room, and putting himself through high school. I ate a lot of bad food and tons of instant soups that I could prepare by warming up water in the microwave. I also struggled to keep any money in my pocket. Between rent and food, making minimum wage did not leave me with much money to help my mother. It almost felt like my money would magically disappear. But whenever I felt like I was not helping my mother enough, I thought of the fact that not being there with my family was an instant savings situation, as my mother had one less mouth to feed. The truth was that life was not easy, and the so-called American dream was nowhere near what I imagined. I was broke, busy, sad, lonely, and my future was enormously uncertain. I lived day by day and survived day by day, but life was only about to get worse.

One Saturday morning, I awakened happy to have a few hours to myself before going to work. I washed my face with cold water and began my walk to the local convenience store where they sold dollar coffee. My friend Carlos, who had ridden his bike to meet me there, walked back with me to the house where we planned to sit outside in the yard to drink our coffee and hang out. It was a perfect California morning with the perfect weather for coffee: not too cold, not too hot. As we turned into the driveway of the house, my aunt and uncle pulled into the driveway at a speed that would signal that they were in a great hurry. For a second, I thought that they maybe needed to take pictures of the house or that my uncle had left a tool behind. I was standing on the passenger side of the truck a couple of meters away when my aunt violently opened the door and charged toward me, screaming, "I knew you would be just like your father, you little thief! Where is the money?" Caught by surprise, I did not step back or move out of her way, which allowed her to grab me by the shoulders and slap me with anger on my left cheek. I remember putting my left hand on my face as I used my right one to keep a distance between us. As I regained stability from the contact and my quick reaction, I noticed that my uncle had exited the truck as well and was charging toward me, swinging a baseball bat. I got so scared that I peed in my pants a little bit and completely froze. By an act of God, when my uncle could have smashed my face, he stopped short of hitting me and began screaming at me instead. It took me a few seconds to understand what was going on. The lady who rented one of the other rooms had called my aunt to tell her that her rent money had disappeared from the house and that I most likely had stolen it.

I could not believe such an irrational accusation. What was worse, I could not believe that my aunt and uncle would believe her. In my mind, it was obvious that she was lying and that most likely she did not have any money for rent after spending it on things like cocaine. But whatever I thought did not matter. All that was important was that my aunt was kicking me out after I had already paid my rent. They both escorted me to the room, where my aunt searched through my folded clothes in my carboard box and even the mattress. My aunt threw my clothes all over the room, making a small mess with the little that I had. They then made me leave, but not before I picked up all my clothes from the floor as my aunt kicked them all to the corner. Needless to say, I begged and cried like a little boy, but they did not care. I had lost all credibility simply by one phone call, and I never even had an opportunity to explain that it was all a lie. It was her word against mine, and my word meant very little. My aunt kept my rent money, claiming that she would have to pay the lady's rent with my money. Broke and devastated with nowhere to go, the first thought that came to my mind was to call Flor.

I had met Flor at a party that some of my friends from school convinced me to attend on a Friday night. It was a warm night and the energy of my young blood kept me going after a long day of work. As far as we knew, the night was young, and the party welcomed us with arms wide open.

The party was full of laser lights moving in all directions, tracing shapes on the walls. There were smoke machines creating a foggy environment that in combination with the flashing lights looked like the perfect setup for a horror movie. However, such stimulation from loud music, lights, and smoke only increased our adrenaline further, making it more enjoyable to be there. There was a lot of drinking, smoking, and fighting going on. There were many people from all different races and ages, all wearing black or dark colors. From the music to the clothing that everyone wore, it was very clear that this was a party for metalheads, rockers, and gothic people. Many of them wore leather pants and jackets along with knee-high leather boots and many other silver-colored accessories. Most guys had very long hair and many earrings, piercings, and tattoos. Both men and women wore heavy eyeliner.

The music was angry, fast, and loud. It was a combination of heavy metal and some rock with enigmatic sounds and orchestral roots that accurately and perfectly fused with fast guitars, reckless drums, and animallike vocal sounds. Strangely enough, even when everyone wore dark clothing, the vibe was bright, and it attracted me greatly. This music was a direct connection to the boy in me who, while growing up, longed for this ferocious rhythm. This was the music and sounds that had not found me in a small town in Mexico, even with Noe's influence. This music, I thought, was written for me. Even worse, in the midst of this chaotic environment, I became angry at the fact that life had deprived me of such a treasure for so many years. Such music was not only a sound or a direct order given by the skilled hands of a musician to their instrument, this music was alive and had a soul of its own, and its soul was malevolent.

I was not only intrigued by the heavy music that I was hearing but by the profile of the many people in there. They all seemed mean and even scary with their dark outfits, but most of all, they all looked free and careless about society's judgment and rules. While their looks were almost intentionally designed to create attention among the public, attention was the least they sought for. Instead, they lived in their own segregated world, fearless and unrestricted by any social norms. Let there be no doubt that there was a layer of anger among many of them, but nothing that I could not match with my own. Let there be no doubt that there was a layer of recklessness and evil, but the music and the environment was a coping mechanism that kept their angry lives in check.

I walked among the crowd with my mouth slightly opened while my mind, as always, paid special attention to the implied life-styles among the many people at the party. They were outcasts by choice and introverts. They were innate artists who clearly knew who they wanted to be by their own voluntary decision and not by any influence of society.

I thought of Victor as I walked through the crowd with the loud music beating in my head. I thought that Victor was one of them. *Victor would belong in a place like this*, I said in my mind. I also thought about the many times I felt confused and out of place about my own personality and taste, but not on that day. That day at that party, I felt like I belonged. Everyone in there was a stranger, yet they were all my brothers and, furthermore, my heroes.

I realize now as I write this book how much of a life-changing moment that day was for me. I had lived my life in search of such freedom. Everything that I had been put through was in preparation for this moment. I could now define who I wanted to be and what I wanted to look like.

At some point during the first couple of hours, my friends and I walked outside the party to meet one of my friend's girlfriends, who had just arrived with some of her friends and was waiting outside by her car. That was when I saw her for the first time. She wore a crop-top shirt that exposed her tanned shoulders and pierced belly button. She wore a tight, long skirt revealing the curves of her hips, and her knee-high boots were meticulously polished. Her curly black hair shone as it reflected away the streetlights on that dark night. Her face was tanned, and her skin belonged to a summer afternoon sitting at a warm beach. Her dark eyes were intriguing and cautious, and the perfectly defined shape of her small lips gave her a thoughtful and attractive look. She acted shy at first and treated me coldly while I struggled to find something coherent to say, but after a while, she laughed at a bad joke that my stupid self was able to put together. Her laughter felt like instant relief to my stressed body, which had tightened up over my relentless effort to grab her attention. She was a humble, caring human being who captivated my heart from the moment I saw her. From that day on, we became great friends. That then led into more. She came to my world to bring color to my life. She was the energy that I did not have and the motivation that I needed to go on.

When my aunt kicked me out of the house, I could not think of a better thing to do but hug Flor and rest my disappointed and saddened body on her shoulder. In a matter of a few minutes, Flor had borrowed her father's truck and had showed up to the rescue. We put my few belongings in her truck and drove away without a direction until we found the nearest park where we parked and talked for hours. Where would I go? What was the best possible solution? Should I just return to Mexico with my mother? Homeless and moneyless, my options were limited. Luckily, my friend Carlos had talked to his mother, who made room for me to sleep on the carpet in one of their rooms in their two-bedroom apartment.

I called my mother a few hours later from a public phone with an international calling card, only to find out that my aunt had called her first and had explained that I was a thief without a future. My mother cried the entire call and begged me to come back. Angry and emotional, I yelled at my mother for the first time in my life, "I AM NOT GOING BACK! I WILL SHOW HER! I DID NOT STEAL ANY MONEY." Once I caught myself screaming and my mother not responding to my rude tone, I felt guilty, lowered my voice and explained to my mother that I would be living with my friend Carlos and his family. "Everything will be okay," I said. "Carlos will let me stay at his house, and I can keep working and going to school." Hesitantly, she agreed and went on to give me advice about respecting Carlos's house. "*El muerto y el arrimado a los tres dias apestan*," said my mother, which is a Mexican proverb that makes no sense when translated to English. However, it means that both the dead and those who are staying with you at your house will begin to stink within three days. My mother was implying that living with my friend was only a temporary solution and that I should work hard at not being noticed in the house. My mother's words of wisdom did not take long to take effect.

CHAPTER 4

San Silvio Park

ONE CANNOT OUTRUN life's seasons. You can try to skip them, but all you are doing is messing with the natural order and postponing the inevitable. I spent my childhood living and thinking as an adult, worried about the source of our meals, the stability of our house, the future of my siblings' lives, and the safety of my family. It was just a matter of time before I not only began thinking like a child but also acting like a child. Just as a child lives only for the moment without any worry about the future, so did I. Just as a child miscalculates decisions and eventually gets hurt, so did I; and just as a child expects forgiveness for his actions without consequences, so did I.

It had been a month or so since I had moved to Carlos's apartment. Really, his apartment was a place for me to shower and sleep. I spent my days working and going to school and my time off with friends, at the local park, and late-night parties. I also saw Flor occasionally, when her parents allowed her to go out. Our main obstacle was that we lived far away from each other and the fact that her parents did not allow her to see any boys or have a boyfriend. I saw Carlos more when I was living in other places than when I was staying in his apartment. My new friends were reckless and immature, but we had music in common, which kept us together and always with a metal or rock band to talk about.

Just like the old proverb says, "Tell me who your friends are, and I'll tell you who you are." My ways began to change. I became extremely irritable like they were, I wore black like they did, and despite how much alcohol had affected our lives, I began drinking and even smoking. What was worse, I began to walk away from God's path. Just like the prodigal son, I ignored the word of God and went as far away from Him as I could. My new friends and their music choice meant more than just a group of teenagers having fun and making mistakes, this music was spiritually dark and called for destruction and recklessness. It also directly challenged God and His divine word. In a very short period, I had entered my rebellious teen-age years with the force of a volcanic eruption, destroying all values and teachings that both my mother and God had instilled in me. I found myself alone and free to steer my life in any direction. There were no rules to ground me or curfews to honor, and I had now cho-sen to ignore God's words, so my future was doomed.

After saving for a few weeks, I was able to buy a five-hundred-dol-lar car. It was my first car, and I was excited to put my Rollerblades away. The car looked just like the price tag, old and cheap. While it was a four-door sedan, only two of the doors opened and matched the color of it. Only one window rolled down, and the trunk had to be held closed with a bungee cord. The inside of the car matched the looks of the outside, with old, dirty, and torn upholstery and a cracked-open dashboard revealing what appeared to be dry, dark-yel-low insulation foam. Only some of the dashboard lights worked, and there was no need for a key to start it. There were a few wires under the steering wheel that had to make contact a few times before the car was on and running. The car even had its signature sound every time I turned and braked. While the car was in bad shape, it was my very first car, and it gave me a feeling of safety and ownership.

Having a car allowed me to get a different job further away from Carlos's apartment that paid a few cents more, which gave me a feeling of progress. It was a warehouse job where I pushed a broom all day and helped unload heavy items from racks. Buying a car was the only thoughtful decision that I had made in a while. Even with a different job, I was not making good decisions with my money or saving anything at all. Many times, I found myself intentionally arriving to the apartment at dinnertime so that I could be offered dinner by Carlos's mother. The truth was that I was not even saving money to eat throughout the week before my next paycheck.

Two months had not passed when I decided to bring Flor and her two friends to the apartment to hang out. Having been there a few weeks had allowed me to feel more comfortable and even part of the family. One of Flor's friends had brought a couple of tequila bottles that we secretly snuck into Carlos's room where we all took turns drinking from it. It only took a few sips for everyone to begin getting drunk and acting a bit louder. Between jokes and tales, a couple of hours went by, and little by little, everyone got more than slightly drunk, at which point Flor and her friends decided to stop drinking.

However, I was not ready to stop. The night was young, there was still plenty of tequila left, and I was feeling more than brave enough to keep going.

I don't remember at what point I lost control of myself, but I recall Flor trying to stop me from drinking, which I disapproved of, violently slapping her hand off the bottle. I was so drunk that the move made me lose balance, and before I could regain my stability, I fell against the window, which could not resist the weight of my body and shattered to pieces. The sound was loud, but the yelling of Carlos's mother was louder and much scarier. Drunk and embarrassed, I was forced by Carlos's mother to clean all the glass off the floor and to leave the house with the little belongings I did not already have in my old car. I got on my knees with my head still spinning and held the dustpan while Flor carefully swept the thousands of glass pieces into it. The worst part is that Carlos's mother demanded an immediate payment of the glass, which Flor had to pay for since I did not have any money. Flor left that night, disappointed, quiet, and unwilling to talk about what had happened.

The next morning, I woke up in my car nauseous, cold, and with a brutal headache. There were clothes all over the seats, and a couple of pairs of shoes scattered about. There were paper wrappers from the uncountable number of ninety-nine-cent chicken burgers I would eat weekly and other trash on the dashboard and middle console. The windows were foggy, so much that I could hardly see the outside. With my eyes barely open, a sick-looking face, and an overwhelming feeling of guilt, I opened the door and managed to hold on to it while I threw up what might have been my breakfast, lunch, and dinner from the day before. I thought about knocking on Carlos's door and apologizing to him and his mother. I owed them so much for letting me stay in their house and giving me all the help that they had offered me. However, I could not find the courage to show myself, and just like a coward, I drove away without a direction and stopped at nearest park.

I did find the courage to call Flor and find out if we were still together. Flor was mad but went to say, "Everyone makes mistakes, and I still love you." I felt so relieved to hear that she was not leaving me. After all, I did not deserve to keep her. I had become the man that I had promised myself I would never become. I acted exactly like the man I hated, and I embarrassed myself and lost the help of a great family. In my mind, I could see my father laughing at me and feel the disappointment of my mother. However, I only had so much time to think about guilt. It was time to face reality and the fact that I did not have any money or a place to go. My car was my new house. In the blink of an eye, I was now a lonely sixteen-year-old teenager putting myself through high school with a full-time job, without any place to live, and broke.

The next few months of my life are hard to recreate. Between school, work, and my daily survival struggle, it seemed like time lost its weight for me and became irrelevant. Each day, I found ways to cope with my reality to the point where every struggle and circumstance was normalized. I became street-smart and found ways to leverage whatever resources I could take advantage of as a homeless teenager. I explored and learned about every gas station in the area. These were great places to rinse, brush my teeth, and get ready for school. I kept a towel in my car and washed my body often wherever possible. I also joined my high school's track-and-field team, which helped me have access to the locker rooms and take warm showers. I learned which streets were safe to park and sleep on and which ones could get me in trouble with neighbors. I watched every student go to and from home and school, while I lived in an old car, which had now turned into my safe place where I could hide from people and the noise around me.

I switched jobs many times and struggled to find any good ones that did not overlap with school. I missed many classes at school to do odd jobs and both arrived late and left early more times than I can count. Life was fast and merciless. It did not care for my circumstances; it did not care for my needs. I sat in my car many times and cried away in silence, forcing my lips together to not scream. Other times I screamed so loud that my head felt like it would explode.

In the midst of my struggle and when life did not seem to give me any breaks, Flor would show up with her innocent smile and do anything she could to console me. She also bought me food enough times for my shame to go away and give in to the one and only solution that I had. Flor was my only support. I remember days when I waited for her impatiently and hungry, knowing that she would feed me and make the time and life pause for a few hours.

As I look back at this season in my life, I know that God placed Flor there to accompany me and support me even when I was not deserving of such a beautiful individual. My life was chaotic and volatile, and my future was more uncertain than the path of a hurricane. Even in my struggle, my stubbornness kept me away from God, who never stopped knocking on my heart. I could hear Him call me out of bad friendships, out of bad places, but I refused to listen. There were days when I became upset at His constant calling and pushed further and further away. I was drinking and partying with the little money I would make and be hungry and broke again and go days with horrible headaches. I could hear God calling my name, and I could see my mother's face of disappointment, but the shame sank me deeper and deeper.

Just when I thought life could not get any worse, my car broke down on the highway on my way to work. Without any money, a phone to call for help, or my so-called friends to help me, I left my car on the side of the road and took as much as I could with me in my school backpack and hands. The car was never insured or registered, so I am sure it was taken away to a junkyard a few hours or days after.

I walked for miles without much direction. I cried for hours until my tears were dry and my uncontrollable hiccups went away. My goal was to get as close to school as possible and to find a place to sleep.

That night, I slept behind the bushes of San Silvio Park but not before having to introduce myself to the homeless people in the park who needed to approve of my stay. One would think that you can sleep anywhere you please when homeless, but things are not that easy. I learned quickly that each park had a different homeless population and that I needed to ask for permission before sleeping over. It is funny how the need for power, hierarchies, and territorial control exist within all social classes. However, Jimmy, the homeless man in charge at San Silvio park, was a kind veteran who simply wanted the park to stay clean. His goal was to keep the police away and be left alone by the locals. He had been homeless at that park for twenty years and had seen it all. He was a tall man, probably in his midsixties, but his long beard kept his face a secret. His green eyes did not belong to his worn-out face. They were bright and healthy. I am not sure if the weight of his heavy blanket or his long gray dreadlocks were responsible for his slouched body or he simply had grown tired of life. Jimmy slept on the cinder block restroom floor, where he did not worry much about the elements. Jimmy carried a long knife on his hips and was not afraid to pull it out. No one ever dared to see whether he was capable of using it or not. Between the war stories, his dislike of government, and his intimidating looks, Jimmy was feared yet loved and respected by the homeless community.

My first night without my car was long and cold. My mind could not find any rest, and I was unable to tune out the many noises surrounding me. My senses were in a stage of alertness to the point where I could hear every leaf move, every cricket sing, the wind, the cars, even the snoring of other homeless people bushes away. I was so alert and scared that I could have heard the steps of an ant walking if there were any around me.

The park was located on the corner of two busy avenues and surrounded by houses and apartments. The back side of it had a long block wall that divided the park from the house's yards. Against the wall, there were several bushes trimmed to knee level with a small open space between the wall and the bushes that was perfect to squeeze in and sleep in. The bushes hid our bodies from the view of the street so well that police and any people driving by would have a hard time seeing us.

My routine did not change much when I lost my car. I slept as much as I could, I showered at school or gas stations, I met Flor anytime she could see me, and I found jobs here and there. I knocked on doors and asked for work; I talked to people and found ways to work at least one day per week. I was able to find a few good jobs that, unfortunately, I had to reject because they would prevent me from going to school. In the back of my head, I always heard the promise that I made to my mother to never abandon school. Keeping this promise gave me some sense of direction. I needed to finish high school before moving on. I could not break that promise.

My other problem was that because of my age, all jobs had restrictions on the number of hours that I could work per week and day. Such restrictions left me with little money to survive. It was then when one of the homeless men told me about a guy who could help me with a fake identification. "I am sure you can pass for a twenty-one-year-old," he said. I am sure that life, even at sixteen, had already traced my battles and decisions on my face, making me look older than I was.

I met a sketchy, paranoid-looking guy at the park, who took fifty dollars that I was able to save with some discipline. The bills were moist from being in my socks, which were a safe place to hide my money when not in my underwear. Life was harsh at the park, and money needed to be hidden. It was not uncommon to see fights between homeless people and stupid teenagers bothering them in their sleep. Money had to be secured at all costs. The paranoid guy took my money and a picture that I was instructed to take at a local pharmacy. When he left, I felt powerless and betrayed. I did not know if he would come back or not, I did not know if he had scammed me and taken my well-earned fifty dollars. Finally, a couple of hours later, he came back with an identification that one would never know was fraudulent. It had my picture, my name, and most importantly, it gave me a date of birth five years before mine, turning me instantly into a twenty-one-year-old.

It was as if the gates of employment had opened for me. I could now find jobs that would give me more than four consecutive hours of work. It was an instant leap into my early twenties, skipping my late teens in a matter of hours. I could also buy cigarettes and alcohol without worrying about being rejected at the counter. It was a crime that had made the life of a homeless teenager much easier; nevertheless, it was still a crime.

CHAPTER 5

La Esquina

As HUMANS, WE are all creatures of habit. Personally, I do well when I find a routine and embrace its daily rhythm. In retrospect, throughout all seasons of my life, including my adolescence, I have worked at finding stability in habits or daily routines. I worked hard at establishing a rhythm of activities that, ultimately, made me feel safe and organized. But never in my life have I experienced more unpredictability in my days than those I had in my late teenager years into my early twenties. Life in this season reached its highest level of chaos, when not a single part of my existence found consistency under any circumstance. Unable to coherently comprehend the conditions under which I lived, like most people, I blamed it on my luck, my destiny, my background, and anything that directly or indirectly surrounded my life. The truth is that yes, I was given the short end of the stick, but my lifestyle did not help my cause. Above all, I was simply the product of all the wrong decisions that I made daily. These actions blinded me and kept me away from the many blessings that God impatiently wanted to pour over my life. It was I who had walked away from God; it was not God who had forgotten about me. As a matter of fact, even when I refused to listen to His calling, He never left my side and worked hard at shaping a bright future for me. Most importantly, He kept me alive through it all.

I was sitting on the corner of my friend's bed, with my hands firmly grasping to the furry bed cover. My hands grasped so hard that my forearm muscles began to fatigue. My mouth was smiling, but my face did not agree with it. I was speaking in a high pitch, using friendly words, yet they were all vague and empty. My words were dishonest and contradicted what I was really feeling inside. I was at a mobile home park, sitting in my friend's room, watching three of the guys that I went to school with get ready for our high school graduation—their high school graduation. Between the transfer from Mexico, having to take a track-and-field class to access the locker room showers, and my full-time job, I was not able to get enough credits to graduate on time. Needless to say, this was a bad day. I saw my high school generation walk to get their diploma from the stands as I prepared for summer school in order to obtain the five credits that I had missed. I named every obstacle that prevented me from reaching my diploma, and I became so angry and frustrated that I told myself I did not even care about it. I thought, *How can everyone else be so lucky?* I saw people screaming and clapping in the stands as each name was called out. I saw mothers cry with proud gestures and tight hugs that stop one from breathing. I saw smiles that fatigue the jaw and walking styles that conveyed pride. All the happiness around me fueled my anger and the blame. Unable to take it anymore, I went to what I then called home: a garage I was renting for a couple of hundred dollars a month.

By the end of high school, I had rented all types of places to live. It all started with my friend's car, which, while uncomfortable, felt much safer than the park. His car was warmer and shielded me from the environment. However, it took me a couple of weeks before I was able to sleep past six thirty in the morning. That was the exact time when the sprinklers at the park would wet any remaining sleeping soul. As much as we hate our alarms, there is nothing harsher than the cold water of a rotating sprinkler. It is so traumatizing that one can develop the habit of waking up before six thirty in one day. I paid my friend fifty dollars per month to sleep in his car, which happened to have tinted windows and hid me from any people walking by it at night.

Not too long after, I rented a room at an apartment complex with walls so thin that I could hear a fart coming from the room adjacent to mine. I can swear that the carpet in that room was more uncomfortable to sleep on than concrete. There was also the obvious invasion of cockroaches that casually walked over my body while I tried to sleep. While all these complaints were manageable and a better alternative than the park, I could not deal with the fact that I was never given a key to the apartment. More than once, I had to sleep outside the front door when no one opened it after I came home late from work or a night out with friends.

There was also the room that I rented at a meticulously clean apartment. However, the owner, a middle-aged single guy with no family, enjoyed walking naked around the house, swinging his Johnson in all directions. I left that one quickly. There was the house with the four loud kids who walked into my room at any time of the day and night to the point that they felt like my roommates. There was the family who rented a room in their apartment but had more rules than a military boot camp. Lights had to be off by 9:00 p.m., no eating in the room, no cooking allowed, no visits allowed, no music allowed, and they even had a "No shirt, no shoes, no business" policy. I left that one quickly as well.

During and after high school, I rented more rooms than I can remember. During this process, I met many people with all types of different lifestyles. I met good and bad families. I saw meticulously clean to crumbling homes. I experienced the complexity of relationships and unique dynamics of each household, and overall, I learned that all families and individuals have their flaws and positive qualities. I tried to see my family in each family whom I lived with and learned that while our lives were not perfect, no one's life was. We all struggle and long for something, we all have problems, and what is worse, in the absence of them, we create them or perceive that we have them.

Right at the end of high school, I was staying at a garage that, so far, was better than any alternative. The garage, while it did not have a shower, came with its own toilet and sink, which felt better than a suite at a five-star hotel. At that point in my renting streak, I was forced to share bathrooms with all types of people, which always felt like sharing a public bathroom. Having my own bathroom was a luxury that gave me a feeling of accomplishment. With such amenities, I was able to surpass the three-month mark, making the garage the longest place I had stayed at in a couple of years.

I had been able to furnish the two-car garage with some items that I had found on the curbside and a comfortable old blue sectional sofa that I found next to a dumpster. On my way home from the graduation, I stopped by the liquor store and bought enough beer to get more than drunk that night. My fake identification had become more than a working tool and was now enabling me to buy alcohol anytime I wanted to. I sat on the old sofa, drinking through the middle of the night, sobbing out of anger and disappointment to the tune of heavy metal and dark music that only fueled my already angry soul.

The morning after, I woke up tired and with swollen eyes to the heat of a metal garage door that daily amplified the outside weather. With a clear mind and no time to dwell on the past, I left the house to go to work. The clock of life never stops ticking, and it was time to move on with my life. That summer I finished my high school education and received my diploma at an empty office with a tired secretary who slowly looked for my name in a cabinet full of diplomas. I thought about the stories behind each of those sacred documents and the many excuses why those people, like me, were not able to finish on time. I thought about the promise that I had made to my mother to complete my education, and for a slight moment, I felt proud of my efforts. The feeling quickly went away when I thought about college and the fact that it would be nearly impossible to attend. I did not have a penny in my pocket or any form of support. With so many obstacles to overcome, I convinced myself that I could wait. I needed to focus on finding a stable job and having the necessary resources in my life to go to college. I even talked to my mother in my mind: *I will go to college later, Mother. Let me get my life together first.*

After that summer, with school over, it felt good to be able to find morning jobs. Life was much easier without having to attend school or do homework. However, the outcome did not change. I was confident that my inability to find a good job was all a result of my school getting in the way of things, but somehow, I found myself struggling to find a good job even after school.

In the years before and after high school, I had more jobs than most people will ever have in their entire lifetime. If you are thinking of a unique job right now, I am pretty sure that I have done it. I worked in all types of warehouses and did everything from shipping and receiving to cleaning and driving forklifts. I packaged, unpackaged, moved, sealed, supervised, folded, scanned, weighed, transported, rotated, tagged, mailed, organized, sealed, built, and oiled more items than I can name. In the restaurant industry, I cooked, cleaned, took orders, served, charged, washed, organized, and did pretty much anything that runs any given restaurant. In the retail industry, I sold clothes, stereos, jewelry, computers, sports apparel, furniture, appliances, vegetables, food, cakes, and cars. In the construction industry, I was a mason, a landscaper, a framer, a plumber, and did any form of labor there is out there. I shoveled, I dug, I demolished; I planted and trimmed trees; I installed and removed floors; I did cabinetry, windows, doors, stucco, painting, welding, irrigation systems, drywall, concrete, rock, and any type of renovation. I drove for a living; I pushed shopping carts at a grocery store; I worked in various hospitality jobs and agricultural jobs. I also sold anything and everything that I was told to sell. I sold CDs and watches at supermarket parking lots, I sat on the side of the road and sold bags of oranges to the passing cars. I sold vacuums door-to-door while I walked miles' worth of neighborhoods. I did any job that crossed me to make an honest living, yet I continued to struggle because of the lack of consistency and my very poor decision-making skills. I went out every time I could, I drank a lot, I partied a lot, and I never planned, not even a day ahead. The little money I made went to my bad habits and was spent with shallow friends. Flor never left my side and continued to feed me and support me whenever she could. Somehow, she could see me through a magic filter that cleaned away my flaws.

There were weeks when I worked at a different job each day, and there were weeks when I did not work at all. The source of the majority of my jobs was *la esquina,* which translates to "the corner."

The corner was a street intersection located in a harsh area of town. It was a corner with a fenced empty lot surrounded by houses that screamed for a renovation or a little bit of attention. The corner was a hub for hundreds of job seekers. The great majority were legal and illegal immigrants who were ready to take on any job and for any amount of money. There were people on the corner at all hours of the day, but mainly in the morning, when contractors and any person with a project in mind could show up and pick up some help.

The process of picking people was far from civilized. Each vehicle rolling by was ambushed by dozens of people, and only the fastest and strongest would get in. It was also a matter of luck because one never knew where exactly a vehicle would pull over. The people standing on the corner easily extended for over one hundred yards, so there were many times when, depending on where one was standing, there was not even a chance at getting into the rolling vehicles. When a vehicle would pull over nearby, the process of getting in the car was aggressive and heartless. Many got punched and pushed and even got their toes ran over by the rolling tires of a scared driver who thought their doors would get ripped off the vehicle. We were all hungry, we were all in need of a job, and proper manners or civil respect were not an option. From a few feet above the ground, we all looked like piranhas attacking a fresh slice of meat that just fell into the water. We were relentless and selfish because we needed to survive.

One never knew what the job was until getting in the car or arriving to the job site. Many of the people picking us up did not speak English or Spanish so we communicated with hand signs. Not everyone was honest either. We all had our one story about the day we went to work and never got paid for our labor.

To most of us, getting in a vehicle was the difference between going back home hungry and having a meal, so the stress was real. Many of the people at the corner had families waiting at home, whether that was somewhere in town, a local park, or back in their countries. The police did not like us standing there and oftentimes would show up to kick us out, but nothing was more frightening than immigration patrols, who would show up silently and by surprise, leaving people running in all directions into traffic and people's backyards.

I woke up many mornings without a cent to eat and dragged myself to the corner with severe headaches. Directly across the corner, there was a little convenience store owned by an old Central American lady who had a huge heart for the many people standing outside. The store was packed with Hispanic products and always smelled like cooked rice. Every morning, she would allow us to drink black watery coffee from a small Styrofoam cup. Each cup was seventy cents, and we all had a week to pay in full. There were many weeks when I hid the furthest away from the store, feeling the pressure of the debt from drinking coffee daily and not having any money to pay for it. There were days when all I had to eat or drink was the seventy-cent watery coffee, the Styrofoam bitten all along the edges.

The corner was a place of sorrow and breaking promises; it was the hidden truth of the American dream. It was a place to gather and find glimpses of hope as dozens of vehicles rolled through every day, leaving the great majority of people standing there waiting for the next vehicle, the next day, the next week, the next trip to the United States. I can close my eyes and see that rusted fence surrounding that empty lot. I can see all the people standing against it with paranoid yet hopeful eyes, restless legs, and their fingers firmly holding to the rusted fence, as if the harder they squeezed it, the higher the chance life would give them an opportunity to prosper.

Some time in my early twenties, I caught a break by finding a job with a construction company that had plenty of work. The job paid good enough to allow me, at times, to save a few hundred dollars in spite of my poor money-managing skills. It seemed as if life had had mercy on me. I was able to pay rent every month on time and even went through a handful of old cars worth no more than a grand each.

Nonetheless, I still faced many hardships and went through times when I did not have any money. The job required that I drive over an hour daily to make it to the job sites, only to work under close to inhumane conditions. We worked in the California desert with temperatures as high as 120 degrees. My malnourished body took the biggest beating ever with full days under the sun and a poor diet. Many times, I went full days on an empty stomach, surviving on cloudy hose water from the newly dug-out wells at the job sites. Other days I begged my way to work. Without any money to eat, I also did not have any money for gas. At risk of losing my job if I did not show up, I packed whatever container I found and stopped by various gas stations, asking people for a little bit of their gas to put in my tank. I did this so many times that I lost the shame in asking for free gas. "Excuse me, sir. Sorry to bother you. I am not asking you for any money today. I just need a little bit of gas to make it to work, and I don't have any money with me. Could you please spare some gas?" I said while I held out an empty milk bottle. My pitch worked most times, and while hungry, I was able to make it from home to work and back. It was not a pretty life, but it felt semistable. Having some job security made my days feel easier and gave me a sense of hope. But this short period was only temporary, and the next hardship was only around the corner.

CHAPTER 6

Cinder Blocks

I WAS SITTING in heavy traffic on my way back home from work. The air conditioner in my newest car, a rusted 1985 Buick, had not worked for the last three owners. In fact, even if it worked, rolling up the windows while the vehicle was on would have been a death sentence. The exhaust pipes were so old that a great part of the smoke filtered up through the floor of the car, which was cracked and rusted too. It was not uncommon to get the floor wet while driving in the rain. The cracks were so wide that water, smoke, dust, and even rocks would get inside the car while I was driving it. I had tried to cover most cracks with duct tape, but the scorching heat of the California desert melted away any of my MacGyver ideas.

I was driving north, which meant that the sun would hit my left cheek with its merciless heat. It was hot, very hot, and the heat opened my pores, allowing all the dry concrete on my face to penetrate them deeper. Each morning, we would plaster our faces with any petroleum-based lotion we could find, but nothing could stop the strength of concrete in combination with excessive sweat and heat. There were days when we plastered our faces with car oil before turning the concrete pump on, all to no avail. We worked one of the hardest jobs there is in the construction field. We sprayed concrete through a high-pressure pump on residential and commercial buildings. The conditions of this job could not be any worse: heavy lifting all day combined with cardiovascular activities that included pulling, jumping, loading, and climbing under high heat and high-pressure sprayed concrete.

I was there because the job paid well, but my body was deteriorating fast. The job itself was a risk to my health, but my lifestyle made everything worse. I was drinking most days and weekends, I was eating poorly, and what is worse, I was not sleeping much.

I arrived at the job site many Monday mornings with my leather pants still on from partying all weekend with zero to a few hours of sleep and a strong scent of cigarettes and alcohol on my breath and clothes. My hair had now reached my lower back, and my face looked much older. There were traces of my lifestyle all over my face, clearly visible to most. While I was in my midtwenties, I could easily pass for someone in my midthirties. I had lost a lot of weight, and while my muscles were very defined from working hard, I looked pale and unhealthy.

By then I had fully joined and embraced what was called a gothic lifestyle. All my clothes were black. I wore many chains around my waist and wrists. I never wore my leather clothes without heavy eyeliner and a touch of white makeup powder to make my face look pale. My fingernails were painted black, and I wore many silver rings in the shape of mythological evil creatures. My face was pierced, and my ear holes were stretched so much that I could fit a cigarette through each of them. I did everything possible to make myself look evil, but the fact was that I did not have to try very hard. I had already reached the furthest point from God and was hanging out with people who were not only atheist but full worshipers of the devil. Their lives, like mine, were dark and angry. They were committed to bashing Christianity and did everything possible to draw the line between God and themselves. Their mouths spoke blasphemy, and their appearance, along with everything around them, was driven by hate and sorrow.

Evil chaos surrounded my life as my bad habits had not changed. I was spending my checks drinking and partying. It was so bad that I was begging for gas to get to work as early as Monday even when I had been paid on Friday. I was counting on Flor to feed me before the weekend was over. Flor was still in my life. She was the one blessing that had not left me. I had failed at everything that I had tried, I could not get out of my own way and lost everything along the way, including my real friends, my integrity, my goals, my purpose. I was floating in a dark place without an orbit, without a direction. I was empty, alone, purposeless, careless, and angry. I was lost and did not want to be found; I was dying but I did not care.

I had even lost the memory of my family, whom I only thought of occasionally. My mother begged me to call her more often than I did, but I was numb to her pain. I did not think of my siblings much and had even forgotten about my father, who a few years back had completely disappeared once again. For all I know, he could have been dead by then, and I simply did not care.

But time would always pause when Flor came to visit. While we no longer had much in common, we could still get along. Flor was almost done with college and lived a purposeful life. She was a dean's list student with a great future. Her life consisted of family, school, and me. She would find any excuse to get out of her house and come visit me. Even while in college, her parents did not allow her to date anyone, so we kept our relationship a secret. We fought many times because of my insensitivity to her life and how much she had on her shoulders. I would demand that she would come see me more often and always screamed at her for not staying overnight with me. I even tried to convince her to move in together when I could not pay the rent of whichever room or garage I was renting. I was clueless about the meaning of commitment and demanded a biased relationship where I did not have to work hard at all. I lied to her so smoothly and guiltlessly most of our relationship. The truth is that I loved Flor, but my immaturity always got in the way of our relationship. I was the stain in her life, and to this day I wonder, Why did she stay with me? Why did she put up with all my chaos when she deserved so much more?

As I look back, the sequence of events at that point of my life is foggy. However, I know that God had tried to call my attention tirelessly. In fact, His calling only grew stronger and more obvious. The closest that I came to listening to His calling was a Sunday morning when I decided to walk into my old church after a night-long party.

I arrived at church drunk, wearing my leather clothes, and with vanishing eyeliner that made my eye bags look darker. The pastor looked at me in the middle of the sermon and called me out in front of the entire congregation and said, "Son, God wants me to tell you that He loves you and that He has never stopped waiting for you to come back." With watery eyes, embarrassed and shaky, I left church in the middle of the sermon.

It was evening by the time I got home. I was wearing a dirty black wifebeater tank top, and my long hair was still humid from my long, sweaty day at work and the long drive back in my boiling car. Even while my windows were rolled down throughout my drive to clear the smoke out of the car, I could still see concrete dust flying in all directions. I was renting a room at an apartment complex. The apartment was on the second floor, and my room had a huge window that faced the road. As I entered the complex and was getting ready to park, I noticed a white vehicle was following me too closely. I did not think much of it, and I parked at the first open spot that I found. As I was exiting the vehicle, the blue lights of the white vehicle, which happened to be an undercover police car, began flashing behind my car. A police officer got out of the car, one hand on his gun and the other on the radio he carried on his chest. With an angry and commanding voice, he asked me to put my hands on the back of the vehicle. Skeptical and finding the situation almost comical, I obeyed.

With a smirk on my face, I asked what the problem was, but his silence was unbroken. He patted me down forcefully as the radio voice gave away my life record. The officer broke his silence only to ask if I lived on the first-floor apartment, claiming that people had seen me in and out of it. I explained that the stairway to my apartment began right at the door of the apartment below, which could easily make it seem like I lived downstairs.

"You don't happen to be friends with those boys downstairs?" he asked with a raspy voice and a playful tone.

"No, sir," I responded with an affirmative tone.

"You would not mind if we take a look in your apartment, right? We are just making sure there is no illegal activity going on like the people downstairs."

"Sure," I said hesitantly and confused.

On our way to the apartment, his demeanor felt friendly and good-hearted. However, when we entered the apartment, his attitude changed completely, and he began searching the entire place frantically, even after I told him that I only rented one room. By then, another officer had arrived and was standing right by the door as if he was sure I was going to run. I was standing in the middle of the living room, from where I could see the destruction transpiring. Even then, I still stood confidently and calmly.

The officer wrecked the place, and without a sign of anything illegal going on, he searched every corner. He emptied drawers, cabinets, searched pockets of both dirty and clean clothes, took cushions out of couches and even flipped mattresses from all beds. For a moment, between the noise of the apartment being searched and the police officer standing at the door, I felt like I was in the middle of an action movie. He was fixated on his task and left the house a mess.

When he was almost done, he began unfolding all my underwear and socks, where he found the fake identification that I had acquired when I was sixteen. Initially skeptical of his searching skills, I could not believe he had found it. My heart stopped beating for a few seconds only to speed up to the point when it felt like it had jumped into my throat.

I don't remember much about the trip to jail, but I remember the feeling. As of that day, I had faced the consequences of my many erroneous decisions, but none of them involved the loss of my freedom. I had been hungry, hurt, alone, and broke but never a prisoner. I always had the liberty of moving anywhere and doing with my life whatever I pleased. This time it was different. I went from having a name to becoming a number.

In jail they took my fingerprints and moved me from cell to cell. I remember hearing many codes and signing papers. There were people screaming and sleeping and telling stories of their past experiences while I, silently and staring at the floor with an empty look, sat on a concrete bench, uncertain of my future. The rooms were white and built with cinder blocks and iron fences that closed with the sound of thunder, locking everything behind it, even the oxygen. There were no windows other than the thin rectangular window on the iron door that faced the hallway where many inmates could be seen walking by. I was afraid, afraid like in the nights I knew my father would arrive drunk and our lives were in danger. I quickly noticed that not everyone in there had been jailed for a petty crime. Most of the guys in there were not fond of the law and the many officers guarding the cells. Some were indifferent about being locked up, and some were proud of it. Others claimed to be undeserving of their arrests, while still others egotistically and arrogantly bragged about every detail of their heinous crimes.

A few hours after checking in, I was stripped naked and given an orange outfit with a pair of sandals. While naked, they robbed me of any pride that I had left in me and took away my dignity as they searched every part of my shaky body, including my anus. I was being moved in all directions and treated like a crash test dummy. I was no longer in charge of my own body.

My walk to the final cell was marked by colored lines on the floor that I had to follow, with my hands folded in front of my pelvis and my head down. I realized that I was not even in charge of my steps anymore. While I walked, I noticed the block walls and thought of the many walls I had built myself and the fact that I never saw them as a prison but as a work of art. How many levels and strings had to be used and whose skilled hands aligned all those blocks together in such a structured way only to incarcerate souls and strip them of their freedom? What I had once seen as a work of art, I then saw as an inhumane practice.

The colored line took me to a cell with many beds. It was the middle of the night by then, and everyone slept. I picked the first empty bed that I found and laid my body down, unable to quiet my mind. I have never cried so much and in so much silence while I bit a towel. I suppressed my uncontrollable cry with so much force that my throat and abs engaged as if I were in the middle of a workout. I was in a cell with many other inmates, and I could not let anyone hear my cry. By then, I had only been there for a few hours, but it was enough to learn that jail was not a place to show any weakness.

It was then that I began crying to God and made promises to Him that I had not made in years. I begged Him to be with me. I repented for the life I had lived all those years. I found comfort in my confession to Him and my begging gave me feel closer to Him. I did not need a solution to my problems, and I did not need my actions to be erased, all I needed was to know that God was with me. I wanted to hear His calling like I always did, I wanted to know that He was with me even when I knew He would not help me skip the consequences of my actions. I could hear my mother's voice clearly, "God forgives, but it is our responsibility to face the consequences."

I ALWAYS HEAR YOUR VOICE, BUT NOW, NOW WHEN I NEED YOU, I CAN'T HEAR YOU! I screamed in my mind with my mouth wide open yet in silence. I looked up to the sky, only to find high metal ceilings that no human being could reach. There was no escape.

Jail for me was a place of reflection and meditation, a chance to assess my actions. It was as if I had not paused to look around for years. I was on the fast track to death, and my trip was reckless. It was so bad that many people who knew me thought I would not even make it to my thirties.

There was a side of me that worked hard at justifying my actions. I said to myself, "I did not kill anyone. I did not rob or hurt anyone. I don't deserve to be here. I only got that stupid identification so that I could work full-time when I was underage." The truth is that I did not feel like I belonged there, which was not a new feeling to me. I was living a life in places and with friendships where I did not belong. The difference this time is that my ability to leave and act at will was taken away from me. Deep in my heart, I knew that I was not there for a false identification. I was there because God ran out of ways to wake me up.

While I could not hear God in jail, for once I could hear my body and my thoughts, and they were both tired of my choices and the conditions under which I lived. In jail, I was given the time and stability to think. The structure that I had searched for to bring consistency to my life had arrived in an unconventional way.

In a strange way, the routine of jail reminded me of the peace that I did not have in my life. It also reminded me that I was not a lost cause. It reminded me of all the work and values that my mother had instilled in me. It uncovered the seed of God that my mother had planted in my heart from the time I was a child. I remembered my struggles, our struggles as a family, the many promises I made my mother, and the one man I promised myself I would never be like, my father.

Jail also highlighted the blessings that had been surrounding me since I had a memory. I was young, I was healthy, and while I had wasted many years of my life on senseless decisions, there were many more years ahead of me. I was a warrior. I had been raised to succeed, and I was not a stranger to hardships. I had been asleep, and it was time to wake up.

While jail was only short term, the legal consequences affected me for years, but its learnings have lasted a lifetime. On my first day out, it only took a few minutes to remember that I had it hard, and there were no more scheduled meals and a roof over my head. Coming out of jail was a new beginning, and once again, I was starting from zero. The difference this time was that I was present and awake, I had a goal, and most importantly, I walked with God.

When I was inside, I lost the little that I had, including my room and car, so I went back to the park where I had once lived. I ran into the same homeless people, including Jimmy, who instantly recognized me and embraced me with a smile from his dirty teeth and his bright-green eyes. The next morning, I was not at the park anymore when the sprinklers came on. I was at the corner before six in the morning, catching an early job. I found myself more aware of my surroundings and joyful to get a job. That afternoon, I ate a warm soup from the corner store and saved the rest of my money. The next morning, I was at the corner at five in the morning. My mindset had changed. I laughed while I was waiting because no matter the outcome of the day, I was free to walk anywhere, to make whatever decision I wanted to make. I was healthy and in search of the one chance that would come sooner or later.

I did not stay at the park very long before an old friend split the rent of one room with me. I was saving money; I was eating well. I even cut my hair short again and was now embarrassed to wear my black leather clothes. I began smiling to people, and people began smiling back to me. I learned that while my face was not the friendliest looking, a face without black gothic makeup would go a long way.

I found a welding job that, while it did not pay much, gave me stability and helped me with structure. Before long, I had a decent car and a more stable life. It seemed like the momentum of a wave pushing toward shore, as I was able to accomplish in a few months what I could not in years. My face was glowing, and my steps were premeditated and goal oriented. I was going to conquer life and reach success at all costs.

Not too long after getting out of jail, I enrolled in a community college. I was so happy to attend my first class that I could not wait to do homework and pulled over on the side of the road to both start and finish it in my car. I began with one or two classes per semester and slowly awoke the intellectual boy in me who loved books, learning, and cultivating the mind. I began writing again, and while I never stopped writing during my years of chaos, this time my writing was hopeful and full of humility and thankfulness.

About a year after jail, my mother called with bad news. My friend Victor had died in a car accident. Her news broke my heart and made life stop for a minute. When I recovered from the shock, I thanked God for Victor's life and promised myself to be the friend who I never was to him. Victor's death was a strong reminder of how blessed I was to be alive. Victor, who had lived a perfect life with a kind heart, was not alive anymore; I, who had wasted years of my life away, was alive and healthy. I promised myself to live a life in his honor, to smile and laugh in his memory like he would have wanted me to. I promised to not disappoint the trust that he had placed in me when he told me that I was born to be great, that I was already great. Victor's death was fuel to my drive, and it humbled my heart greatly. After I hung up the phone, I could have run a marathon or I could have climbed a mountain without any fatigue, but instead, I sat alone in silence, framing my thoughts and consoling my heart. It was time to move on.

Flor and I were still together for a couple of years after jail, and we had finally moved in together. At first, our economic struggle was smaller than any relationship hardship that we faced. When we finally reached stable days, we realized that we had grown apart. We were no longer the two teenagers who laughed and paused time with never-ending conversations while we listened to rock music. We were fighting a lot and could not get along anymore. She was a beautiful person then and always, while I had lived an unpredictable life. I had endured in a matter of a few years what many never will or what others will take a lifetime to experience.

The truth is that I had fixed some areas of my life but still needed work in many others, and my still-immature self could not find the words and actions to keep us together. A part of me will always ask the what-ifs: What if I would have been a better man? What if I would have invested more time into trying to understand her needs? What if I would have tried to speak her love language? What if I would have been less selfish? I cannot change what I did in the past. However, there is one thing that I am certain of: God placed Flor in my life to remind me of all the good there is in this world during a time when I spent my days angry at my circumstances and always blaming others. God blessed me through her compassion and her laughter. She was the only light that brightened my days for many years; she was God's instrument of love and help. When I was the furthest from God and did want anything to do with Him, He was always near me through Flor.

CHAPTER 7

The Sign

IT WAS THE land of the four seasons, where winter selfishly stretches its arms over spring and fall, and summer is like a drop of sweet honey on your mouth that quickly melts away, leaving you addicted to its taste. The land of magnificent trees that endure the weather of each season and each of their hardships. The land that gave birth to America through a story of resilience, faith, and sorrow. It was this same land that on a late New England summer day in the early eighties welcomed the life a beautiful baby girl with eyes the color of a morning summer sky. Her birth abundantly showered her parents with joy as they impatiently waited to see her face for the first time. She was born in a household full of love, culture, and discipline and with parents whose marriage was as strong as the roots of the matured trees that surrounded her beautiful house.

Born with the innate psychology of an athlete and the discipline of a studious child, her choices and lifestyle, from the time she developed the use of reason, were thoughtful and premeditated. While an only child, her childhood was surrounded by the company of friends and neighbors who felt just like family. She grew up happy and with parents who sheltered her with love and worked hard at instilling their wisdom in her.

Her first hardship hit her life when she was only ten. Her mother, an inspiring woman, sports coach, and teacher by trade, faced the spread of a deadly medical condition that miraculously did not take her life. The stress and anxiety that she felt for the two years that her mother was suffering made something very clear to her: she was not in control. Between her tears and her father who cried by her bed in silence while she pretended to sleep, she could hear the presence of God and angels by her side. She could not name the feeling yet, but deep inside, she felt the calmness of the spirit of God who watched over her and her father, a man with a humble heart of gold.

Grateful for the blessing to keep her mother by her side, these two years were the foundation of her faith in the Lord, whom she would later be able to define and follow. God had showed her that while her life had been nearly perfect, hardships could arise at any moment. From that time on, she learned to appreciate the abundance of stability and love and the teachings that adversities bring to our lives. She learned that life did not owe her anything and that everything she had was given and could be taken away by God at any moment.

During her teenage years, she was a role model in sports and school, excelling in everything she was involved in. Her room had more trophies and medals than she could display and awards that most people can only dream to receive. With colleges lining up and fighting over an opportunity to have her join them, a reminder that she was not in control hit her life again when she tore a ligament in her knee and saw all her scholarships fading away. After surgery, she shed many tears as she sat on the couch of her living room, watching her athletic dreams wash away. But her circumstances were no match to her faith in God and her resiliency, which brought her back from the ashes and placed her in a prestigious college, where she took on a different sport, conquered it, and became an All-American. Once again, she had faced a hardship and came out stronger and full of wisdom.

After college, she found herself lost and uncertain about her next steps. She took on a few jobs here and there, pushing paper or working with spreadsheets, which she hated greatly. Deep in herself, she knew she was born for something better and she would not stop until she found her destiny. It was then when she made one of the most drastic decisions of her life: to move away from home and begin her second bachelor's degree to pursue a medical career.

Her hair was the color of sunshine, with curls that could only be made by the talented hands of a sculptor. Her big blue eyes were like shiny marbles sprinkled with different shades of light hazel and green. Her tall and athletic body made it seem as if she had escaped a display window from an expensive boutique store. Her steps were confident yet humble, and her face would make even the grumpiest person alive smile. Under the California sky, her new home, her pale face glowed as her skin took on a different shade that made her look healthier and even happier.

She plastered her face with sunscreen as she rode her bike for hours and miles along the beautiful beaches of California. Her move to this new state was not premeditated. By the time she finished college, she had dated a guy for a few years who was from the Golden State. Her plan was to change her career and stay close to him in the process of going to school. While her relationship with him was solid, he was not a man of faith, which left a void in her that she tried to ignore for years, but it had only grown bigger and heavier. She spent many nights thinking about her future life with him and the dynamics of a household where she could not share her faith with him or her children. Each time she thought about it, she abruptly stopped herself as, knowing he would never change, there was only one solution. Instead, she asked God for a sign. She wanted God to show her the way, and she knew that sooner or later God would lead her in the right direction as He always had.

For her new degree, she was forced to take a couple of general classes at a university of her choice. She fought this prerequisite with everything she had but was not able to have it waived. Unhappy about it, she searched every possible school in the area but was unable to find the classes she needed. Stressed out but determined to get it done, she found a small community college where she could take these classes and move on to her new career. She would go from an elite university to a small community college in a southern California town.

* * *

I was running late from work, and my class had already started. It was my first class of a new semester, and I was going to be late. I had done everything possible to get out of work on time, but it was not possible. I had been in college for a few years, but I only had a few classes under my belt. I was working fifty to sixty hours per week and taking no more than two classes per semester, so I was not finishing college anytime soon. I also had a new job working at an insurance agency. Miraculously, I had been able to land my first office job. Sitting in my car after I had been laid off from welding, I saw a post on a local magazine that said, "We are hiring salespeople." Sales was only one of the skills in my repertoire, so I quickly called for an interview.

The morning of the day of the interview, I landed a job at the corner and dug trenches all day long. By four o'clock, I was ready to be interviewed at an office with people acting as if they have had too much coffee. There were many people on their phones speaking and typing loudly on their keyboards. They all wore suits and ties and laughed nervously and loudly as they uttered words like "premium" and "coverage" and "accidents." I quickly realized that this was a job in demand, as there were more than a handful of people interviewing for it. I also realized that I was the only one without a résumé and wearing ripped jeans and a pair of shoes full of mud. I was not shaved, I smelled like sweat and grass, and my shirt had sweat stains on my chest and armpits.

With a knot in my throat, I stepped to the desk where people were being interviewed by a guy in a suit with a crooked smile. With broken English and embarrassed of my appearance, I introduced myself and kept eye contact. Surprisingly, he did not seem to notice my appearance and acted as if he did not care about it. I even made a comment about going to work that morning, but he ignored it. His only question was "Can you sell?" to which I responded, "Sir, I have sold anything that has crossed my way, I have sold CDs, oranges, vac-uums, clothes, furniture, construction contracts, food, books, shoes, and probably more things that I don't remember at this moment." He did not seem shocked by the long list, and taking off his watch, he asked how I would sell the watch to him. Frankly, I don't remem-ber my exact words, but I know that I had sold watches in supermar-ket parking lots, so the scenario was not new except that it meant I could get a job. I left the interview certain that I would not get the job, but after a daily relentless follow up by phone, I was hired two weeks later as an insurance agent at a time in my life when not even my personal vehicle was insured.

I arrived at my class late, and with a blushed face, I found the first empty chair to sit. I was wearing loud dress shoes that did not help my quiet entrance and too much cologne—so much that I am sure the small class of twenty or so smelled my arrival. That was the first time I saw her blue eyes. She wore an ugly sweater that looked like a small blanket around her chest, and her messy curly hair was gorgeous. Sitting directly across from me, she looked at the teacher very attentively while I looked at her every move and ignored every-thing the teacher said. I noticed she seemed bored to be there, and I could tell her hands were cold by the way she hid them under the gray sweater. I thought, *What would a guy like me need to do to catch just a little bit of her attention?* But lacking confidence and aware of my background, I thought that there was not a remote chance that she would look at me.

A few weeks went by, and I did not give much thought to her presence in class. It was as if I had lost a battle that I did not even dare to fight. Truly, I was intimidated by her beauty and unique looks. I had also just gotten out of a relationship that I was not mature enough to save, so what were the chances that I could start another one and be successful at it? One Thursday evening, I was running late to class yet again. I ran through the hallways of the building with my loud shoes only to learn that the teacher was late and the classroom was locked. A group of students waited by the door, and others went home immediately. I stood by the door, happy to not be late, when I realized that the blue-eyed girl was standing next to me.

Stupefied by the fact that she was standing there literally rubbing my shoulder with hers, I thought of anything that I could say to start a conversation. A few seconds went by when I noticed she carried a cycling water bottle, so the first words that came out of my mouth were "Do you ride?" to which she replied with a smile, "Yes, I do. My name is Claire." We made small talk before I asked, "Would you like to ride sometime?" and she responded, "I would love to."

During my first year of college, I had met a guy who practiced cycling. The first time I saw him wearing spandex, I made fun of him and told him I would never wear a pair of those. A full semester after, we were both riding together as I fell in love with the sport. With a little bit more stability in my life, I had been able to buy a nice bicycle on credit that cost me more than many of the cars that I have had. Cycling was therapeutic to me and a way to clear my mind. I was riding miles and miles every day, getting better by the mile.

A few weeks after that evening, we had our first ride together. We talked for hours as we suffered through the pain of a thirty-mile mountain climb. She was so fit and strong that there were moments when I thought I would fall behind, but my body was floating on clouds while I talked to her and the endorphins of the workout increased even more every time I made her laugh. Her personality was calm like the water of a peaceful creek running through a valley, and I saw my stress wash away in her presence and my laughter amplify. I wanted the mountains to be higher and our bicycles to go slower. I did not want our ride to end. In my mind, I was certain that this ride was the closest I would ever get to her. When our ride ended, I needed an excuse to see her for a little bit longer, so I asked if she wanted to go eat, to which she agreed.

We were at a Mexican restaurant ordering tacos and sodas when it dawned on me just how much more beautiful she was this close up. I took a deep breath and once again reminded myself that I was thinking about something impossible and, more importantly, something that I was not deserving of. When we sat at our table to eat, I bowed my head and prayed before we ate our meals, thanking God for the food and the ride together. Little did I know that a brief prayer would change my life forever. I learned later in my relationship with

Claire that, even when we did not start dating until many rides after, it was that one prayer that made her pay attention to me. It made her feel like she was home. For years, she had asked God for a sign that would help guide her in finding the right spouse. My prayer was the sign that she had been seeking. Years later, it was on that same mountain where I got down on my knee and proposed to Claire.

* * *

Children, is there anything impossible to the power of God? No, there is not. Your mother and I were born thousands of miles apart in completely different environments. Our backgrounds could not be any different. Our cultures were so different we did not even speak the same language for most of our lives. But we had the mercy of God in common, and from the time we were born only three days apart, He had traced a path that would bring us together. Our hardships and our triumphs were different, but they all led to the word of God.

When I played soccer on the poorly paved streets of Mexico, your mother played soccer on beautiful flat grass, but the joy of the goals we both scored felt the same. When she struggled with her mother's battle with death, I struggled with my father's addictions and our scarcity at home, and both situations were painful. However, God was always by our side. When I struggled on the streets of California and lost my way, your mother dealt with the disappointment of her injuries and losing everything that she had worked hard for. In the end, God was shaping our characters and preparing us for the miracle of finding each other among the millions of people in this world and across the thousands of miles that separated us our entire lives before the day we met. There is no rational explanation for your mother and me meeting but the perfect will of God.

CHAPTER 8

Eyes on Him

WE WERE SOMEWHERE in the Colorado mountains, on our way to the land of the trees. It was only our second day on the road, and we had already past the *Sin City*, Vegas, and the long valleys of Utah. We had quit our jobs and given away everything we had, carrying only our dog and anything we could fit in our car. We were on our way from California to the opposite side of the country and ready to begin a new life.

They say marriage is a compromise, but up to that point, it felt to me like I had not compromised much. Our lives were perfect and stable without a trace of hardship or regret. Her calm and happy personality had balanced anything that needed work in me. Her confidence in me made me feel like a superhero. I could do anything; I could be anything. She saw potential in me that no one had ever seen, and she believed that I could achieve anything.

In California, we had a small one-bedroom apartment with some furniture, our plant Matilda, our dog Rufo, and our two bicycles. We did not need much other than each other and the word of God that was leading our lives. We both had good jobs and a schedule that allowed us to spend time together. After much effort, I had been promoted to a great position in an insurance company, and Claire had graduated and now worked at a renowned hospital in Southern California. Moving our lives away and leaving everything behind felt like the first huge compromise to me, but I trusted Claire and the plan that God had for us.

The process of adjusting to a new place was not easy, but everything seemed to perfectly fall into place. I found a great job with another insurance company only a couple of months later, and Claire had job offers from the six places where she interviewed. Only a month after we had arrived, while we were staying with my in-laws, we learned that we were pregnant. As a joke, we can say that we found out about it at a time when we were homeless and jobless. However, knowing the true hardships of a homeless life, I am certain that we were not remotely close to such harsh circumstances.

By the time our son was born, we had bought our first home. It was a modest three-bedroom home surrounded by skyscraping trees and a long gravel driveway. We were so happy to receive our first child into this world in a place of our own and with a stable life. I was given a chance to be the father I never had and have the family that I only dreamed of. There were many nights when I stared at the size of those small baby hands and wondered at the miracle of life and the blessing of being a father.

Three years after, we were pregnant again, and the blessings continued to pour. We now had a different house in an affluent community with houses that cost more than one hundred houses all together from the place where I was born. Claire went back to school to further her education and, with incredible effort, received her third degree while nursing our first baby. I also earned various promotions and continued to climb the corporate ladder at a pace that most people will never see in their lifetimes.

By the time our baby daughter was born, I had been in school for almost ten years. Between early life circumstances and now my children and my job, I always took one or two classes per semester, which delayed my ability to finish college. Nevertheless, I was on a journey to finish my education. I was on a journey to conquer this world, and all my efforts and discipline were paying off. Eleven years and three different schools after, I graduated with a degree in business. Unlike most, I had done things backward, and by the time I was out of school, I already had a dream job. Finishing school was the end of a long journey that demanded a level of discipline that I never thought could be possible to achieve. I worked during the day and studied during the night, all while my family was growing. My weekends were full of homework and carried the burden of school responsibilities day after day. However, I always had Claire with me, who made me feel invincible and supported me all the way through.

One winter morning, my phone rang on my way to work. The number seemed to be from Mexico, so I answered quickly, thinking it could be my mother or any of my siblings. A faint voice spoke after a few "hellos" on my side without a response. "Hi, son," said the voice that I had never forgotten about, my father's. I could not respond for a few seconds. The battle between my heart, my mind, and my tongue could not be settled fast enough to answer my father's greeting. "Hello," I said, incredulous of such a moment. His call had come to me like a bucket of cold water being poured over my shoulders. It was not that I never expected to talk to him again but how busy life had been all those years and how little I had thought about him. With broken words and a weak voice, my father explained that he was calling to say goodbye. He was sick and on the verge of death. He was somewhere in southern Mexico, in a rural city. He had wasted his life away until the day he fell sick without any resources, alone, and without anyone to help him. Without any pride left in him and counting the days before his death, full of regret and sorrow, he was calling his children to ask for forgiveness. Many thoughts went through my mind at that moment, and most of them were ungodly, but my heart melted quickly at the tone of his voice and the end he was facing. I thought about how much he had taught me through his actions. He was the example of the life I should not live. I remembered the many mistakes I had made early in my life and felt closer to him in a strange way. I was crying as I heard his last words, and with an honest heart full of sorrow for the father I could not have, I realized that I did not hate him anymore. I did not feel any resentment toward him. I freed myself of the angry feelings that I carried on my shoulders. Many years ago, I realized that I had the power to shape my own future, to make my own decisions. I no longer needed to be defined by my father's actions and the impact that he had on my life. I was freed by the grace of God, and all the hardships that he imposed on me had made me who I am today. I did not regret anything, and therefore, I did not blame him for anything anymore. I had forgiven him. When our call ended, I felt like a missing part of my heart had been filled, and I felt full. I thanked God for the gift of forgiveness and the opportunity to be the father that I never had.

Time passed, and my life battles were miniscule compared to the blessings surrounding my new life. My battles were no longer life-threatening or essential for survival. Instead, they were vague, imaginary, and more often than not, vain. *Should I buy that motorcycle? Do I need a new suit for the upcoming meeting? I can't believe they cannot deliver our food on time! Should we take a vacation to Florida or North Carolina?* I did not worry about food or clothing anymore, and shelter went from being a daily struggle to an expensive mortgage. My children were healthy and happy, with every single one of their needs taken care of. They were surrounded by toys, shoes, clothes, and the many materialistic factors that make parents proud to be able to offer their children. My wife loved me greatly, and our marriage was almost too perfect to be true. We had submitted ourselves and our marriage to God, and He had done miraculous things with our lives. I spent my days counting our blessings and questioning God about His reasons for picking me as the recipient of this perfect life. Our lives were abundant in every single area: money, health, careers, our daily routine, and our beautiful children. There was not a single loose end. God had crafted the perfect plan for my life, and every single struggle and every single circumstance that I had been exposed to was merely a step toward the construction of this perfect life and this state of nirvana.

I was the perfect picture of the American dream. An immigrant who had come to this country, adapted, learned the language, became educated, landed the executive job, married his beautiful wife, had healthy adorable children and was supposed to live happily ever after. But at night and when I found myself alone without the noise of the kids or the daily responsibilities, or when I simply found myself in silence with no one to disrupt me, I felt overwhelmed with guilt. I could not be the one chosen for this blessing. There were many others who had also worked hard and had not even accomplished half of the things I had accomplished before my midthirties. I did not deserve this life. Why me? Why this abundance and peace?

When all the survival battles had ended, there was yet the biggest battle to fight: the battle of my mind. It was like I held back all this pressure and anxiety, from the time I was a little boy, as I fought in life and pushed through doors with a relentless drive. I violently grabbed life by the neck and demanded my share, and I had used God's mercy to guide me and bless me over and over again. But when there was nothing else to fight, nothing else to worry about, all my memories haunted me.

After the many mistakes I made early in my journey, I had lived my new life aiming at perfection, success, and stability. However, when I succeeded in reaching my goals, I did not know how to deal with such overwhelming success. I found myself feeling purposeless and empty. There was simply too much peace in my life, and in the absence of conflict, my brain began to create imaginary problems that my chess-player mind always viewed as a catastrophic future. And one day, when the many thoughts, guilt, and pressure that I had put on myself could no longer be handled by my mind, I broke down. I was overwhelmed with anxiety and worry about the most irrational things.

My mind had gone through years of an incessant fight-or-flight mode, so long that I was unable to disengage from such a frantic state. I began to panic about little things and small problems or issues at work or at home because the bigger imaginary problems had overwhelmed my mind. I could not relax nor let go of absurd catastrophic thoughts. While I had claimed to be a man of faith all these years, I was now afraid of death more than ever. The thought of not being able to see my kids grow old hunted me down. While peace, love, and stability surrounded my life, I saw the world collapse around me, my heart would race, and my head would spin. I was sure that the oxygen that I once inhaled innately would no longer keep me alive as the accelerated rhythm of my heart choked me and killed me violently. I could not catch my breath. There was a battle in my mind, forcing my body to dwell in an imaginary dying state even when the world around me stood still and my health was intact.

Sometimes, even with everything I had to live for, I found it hard to get out of bed in the morning. It was a new type of hardship, one that could not be conquered without facing my past and the damage that my childhood and teenage years had done to my mind. It was time to focus the fight on me and no longer on the world. It was my powerful, determined, driven self against me. I was my own enemy to battle, and I had never been more scared of anything or anyone.

In the next months, I bent my knee to pray more than I had done in years. Through prayer, I realized that God had become a tool in my life—a tool that had helped me accomplish my dreams. I had forgotten about God yet again. This time I was not in bad company, homeless, or living a dark life. This time it was different—I had used God to my convenience. I had been wise in my own eyes. This time around, God had taught me another lesson by surrounding me with everything and anything that I had ever dreamed of: happiness is not found in success or in any of our dreams if we forget to prioritize the Lord.

* * *

Children, I did not begin writing this book with this end in mind. Instead, my goal was to show you the hand of God in my life. I wanted to teach you perseverance, hard work, patience, determination. I wanted you to keep my memories next to your heart so that when I am no longer here in flesh, I can still parent you in my writing. Yes, that is selfish of me, but like most parents, I wanted you to learn from my mistakes, to appreciate everything you have been given and to honor God with all your heart and soul. The happily ever after end of this book can exist in your life and my life, but never without the natural hardships that life places in front us. Such hardships are life's best teachers and God's shaping tools for our characters.

Perhaps God wanted you to know that happiness is not found in success, meeting goals, accumulating the riches of this world, or living a perfect life. Peace of mind and spirit along with happiness of the heart lies in realizing that we are not in control of our lives and that as much as we plan and hope for, God will always have the last word.

Work hard and build and accomplish your goals, but never take your eyes off the Lord, or your success will be empty.

God has blessed me with these fingers and this mind that, working in concert, have put these words on paper to tell you to prioritize Him over all your dreams. Make God the commander of your wars, make Him the center of your life, and you will be blessed with more than what this world can offer us. God will bless you with peace and joy.

Not once, the riches of this world and the many accomplishments that He allowed me to reach fulfilled me. In response to that, I kept wanting more, asking for more. God has the right way of teaching us about life and simply kept helping me with every goal I had planned to meet. God does have a sense of humor. I am sure He smiled as He saw me take my eyes off Him, use Him as a tool, succeed, and still find myself empty.

Success in life is about loving and being loved, is about each smile of the day that overwhelms our souls with laughter and peace. Success is being able to pause life, breathe, and pay attention to the details that matter around us. Life is about the blessing of facing struggles and difficulties throughout any season so that we learn to appreciate each breath and stay humble. True success is not about reaching your goals but about never running out of them and enjoying every journey. You will always run out of materialistic goals because they are all achievable. Instead, make it a goal to love and give to others, to teach those who need teaching, and to listen to those who need to be listened to. Success is about finding happiness in both scarcity and in abundance, because your eyes are not focused on how much you have but how much you appreciate the little or the much that has been given to you. Success in my life was about being present in each minute of your lives without dwelling in the past or worrying about the future. Make it a goal to pursue the word of God, which will never stop pouring wisdom into your lives.

Face life's hardships with a smile, and give control to the Lord, whose plan is to mold your future in a precious way. Life is as complex and beautiful as a chess game—build your strategy with the word of God, and let His love guide your every move.

Lastly, let me thank you for the light you have brought to my life. We teach our children how to live life; in return, they teach us the meaning of it.

Love,
Papá

ABOUT THE AUTHOR

JESÚS ZUBIATE IS silent writer of many blurbs about life and spiritual themes. After more than two decades writing poetry and nonfiction for his own circle of friends and family, Jesús writes his debut novel for his children, *Love, Papá*. A teacher's son, Jesús grew up in northern Mexico, under the merciless Chihuahuan desert heat in one of the poorest areas of the state. A victim of home violence by his drug addict father, Jesús found peace and shelter in the art of writing as pen and paper, with his mother's career, were never scarce around his humble house. In early childhood, Jesús won every poetry, public speaking, and writing contest he could enter. His innate ability to transfer thoughts onto paper, inspired by the sorrow of a broken household, showed early signs of a career in writing. Today, Jesús resides in the northeast with his wife and two children. Inspired by memories of hardships and resiliency from his childhood, Jesús writes his first published book—his most inspiring story yet—*Love, Papá*.

CPSIA information can be obtained
at www.ICGtesting.com
Printed in the USA
BVHW080957310321
603803BV00001B/7

9 781662 431036